A Merciful God

"Reb Levi Yitzhak of Berditchev" (Pen and Ink) by Netanel Miles-Yépez ca. 2002

A Merciful God

Stories and Teachings of the Holy Rebbe, Levi Yitzhak of Berditchev

Third Expanded Edition

Translated and Retold
with Commentary by

Zalman Schachter-Shalomi
& Netanel Miles-Yépez

Albion
Andalus
Boulder, Colorado
2024

*"The old shall be renewed,
and the new shall be made holy."*
— Rabbi Avraham Yitzhak Kook

Albion-Andalus Inc.
P. O. Box 19852
Boulder, CO 80308
www.albionandalus.com

Design and composition by Albion-Andalus Books
Cover design by Hauke Sturm
Cover illustration by Netanel Miles-Yépez

ISBN: 978-1-953220-34-9 (Hardcover)
ISBN: 978-1-953220-35-6 (Paperback)

Manufactured in the United States of America

In loving memory of Miriam bat Sarah

As God is merciful, so shall you be merciful.
— Talmud (Shabbat 13b)

For my daughters,
Miriam, Tina, Lisa, Shalvi, and Rosi
— Z.M.S-S.

For my nieces,
Virginia and Jada Rose
— N.M-Y.

May they contribute their own understanding
to the "White Letters of the Torah."

Contents

Acknowledgements

I wish to give a heartfelt thank you to all who helped us with this book: first and foremost Rabbi Sarah Leah Grafstein, whose generosity made the first printing possible; Rabbi Ruth Gan Kagan, who read and made suggestions on the manuscript, providing various sources for it; Rabbi Bahir Davis, who worked on early versions of some of the stories and teachings; Daniel Jami', who proofread and made many helpful suggestions for the third edition; and my wife, Jamelah.

— N.M-Y.

Preface to the 1st Edition

This small collection of teachings and stories actually began as a chapter in our book *A Heart Afire: Stories and Teachings of the Early Hasidic Masters*; but for reasons of size and continuity, it was cut from the final manuscript. This was a great pain to us, as Reb Levi Yitzhak communicates the spirit of Hasidism in a way that few other Hasidic masters could: his expansive personality was able to forgive his fiercest enemies, to bring factions together, and to say the unsayable of his time. For all of these reasons, we are particularly happy to be able to bring out this small collection for all those who already love Reb Levi Yitzhak, and for those who are waiting to be introduced to him.

Completed in Boulder, Colorado, on the 25th of Tishrei, the 200th anniversary of Reb Levi Yitzhak's passing.

— Zalman Schachter-Shalomi
& Netanel Miles-Yepez

Preface to the 3rd Edition

It is a personal joy to see this work re-released in a new expanded edition almost fifteen years after its original publication. This is particularly true because *A Merciful God* was the first book published by Albion-Andalus Books, and the reason I created the publishing house in the first place.

As noted in the original preface, it was meant to be a chapter in our book *A Heart Afire;* but, needing to reduce the size of that very large book for the publisher, it was cut as the most stand-alone chapter in the book. Being sad that I had to cut the chapter, and disappointed with a number of experiences I had had with various publishers,

A Merciful God

I decided to form my own publishing house and publish this book myself, remembering that Schocken Books used to publish wonderful short works like Martin Buber's *Ten Rungs* and *The Way of Man*. Perhaps somewhat naively, I hoped that this book might have a place among such works.

Now, ten years after Reb Zalman *z"l*'s passing, I am happy to see it coming out again in a new and improved version (as the first edition was typeset in Microsoft Word on my computer)! I would like to thank properly Rabbi Sarah Leah Grafstein who, learning what I was attempting to do all those years ago, sent me $600 to get started. It was enough, and Albion-Andalus Books was always 'in the black' thereafter. Thank you, Reb Sarah Leah.

— Netanel Miles-Yepez
  July 3rd, 2024

Note to the Reader

This work is a collaboration between two authors, and thus raises certain questions with regard to 'voice' in its commentaries. Since this is a subjective and personal book, a first person voice creates a mental continuity for the reader. In most cases, we do not call attention to which author the pronoun 'I' refers, finding it largely irrelevant to the subject, and knowing that is common agreement between us about the opinions and views included in the work.

As much as possible, we have also attempted to use gender-inclusive language throughout, even bending the rules of grammar and historical accuracy on occasion to do so. These stories and teachings come from a culture and a time when the masculine 'he' was thought to include and encompass the feminine 'she.' Without making any value judgments about that time, we must nevertheless speak to the more diverse audience of today, and for the needs of our own time.

— Z.M.S-S. & N.M-Y.

Prologue

Reb Levi Yitzhak of Berditchev is one of the most celebrated and beloved of all Hasidic rebbes. Though possessed of a luminous intelligence, the Berditchever demonstrated little attachment to his great intellectual abilities. If he could have sold them to buy a pure heart and justice for his people, he surely would have. Thank God, he was never asked to make such a bargain; for his brilliant mind was put into the service of his pure heart, and the result was a legacy of the utmost holiness and compassion. Thus, this genius of Torah is generally considered the warmest and most accessible of all Hasidic rebbes.

Beginnings

On the day Reb Levi Yitzhak was born, the holy Ba'al Shem Tov called his disciples to a celebration. The disciples rejoiced, eating and drinking with the master; but no one knew the reason for their joy. Finally, the Ba'al Shem Tov explained, "Today, a holy soul has entered the world, a soul who will stand and defend all of Yisra'el."[1]

Reb Levi Yitzhak's father, Rabbi Meir, a noted talmudist and kabbalist, was the Rav of Husakov in Galicia, and descended from a long line of rabbis. His mother, Sarah, was known for her piety and wisdom, and was likewise of a distinguished lineage, being descended from the famous commentator on the Talmud, Rabbi Shmuel Edels (1555-1631).

Being raised in this atmosphere of piety, studying Talmud and Codes with his learned father, Reb Levi Yitzhak's own gifts soon began to shine. Before long, he was sent to continue his education in Yaroslav, where he became known as 'the genius of Yaroslav.'[2]

At seventeen, Levi Yitzhak was acquired as a son-in-law by Yisra'el Peretz (one of the principal supporters of the *yeshivah* of Libertov) for his daughter, Perl; for in Eastern Europe, at that time, wealthy fathers were known to seek brilliant and pious young scholars as husbands for their daughters. Therefore, thanks to his father-in-law's support, Levi Yitzhak was free to continue his studies of Talmud and *kabbalah*. Nevertheless—and much to his new father-in-law's *chagrin*—another interest began to take hold of the young Levi Yitzhak.

Near Libertov was the town of Ritchovol, where the great scholar Shmuel Shmelke Horowitz (1726-1778) of Nikolsburg was head of the *beit din* and the *yeshivah*. Levi Yitzhak implored his father-in-law to give him leave to study under the great man in Ritchovol; but his father-in-law objected. It is possible that Reb Shmelke's association with the Hasidic movement and its leader, the Maggid of Mezritch, was the reason for Yisra'el Peretz's objection. Still, Levi Yitzhak was determined and fasted in protest until his father-in-law finally relented.

Having obtained this permission, he then traveled to Ritchovol, where he was soon introduced to the way of Hasidism by Reb Shmelke. It is likely that Reb Shmelke then took the brilliant young man to Mezritch to introduce him to the Maggid personally.[3]

Divine Games

There is no tradition of Reb Levi Yitzhak's first meeting with the Maggid of Mezritch; but we do have a wonderful record of a personal conversation between the Maggid and his young Ḥasid, as it is preserved in Reb Levi Yitzhak's journal.

I asked my *rebbe* if playing 'games' or 'practical jokes' *(sha'shu'im)* was the same as lying. He responded: "Practical jokes can be true; for God commanded Avraham to offer Yitzhak up, but had no intention of letting him be slaughtered . . . only to be 'offered' or 'raised' up in exaltation. (Gen. 22:2)[1] Avraham, however, in preparing the offering, did not realize that a practical joke was being played on him."

This is wonderful; for how often do we get to hear the kinds of questions the great disciples asked their rebbes in their youth, or what issues they were struggling with? Of course, one could see the young

Reb Levi Yitzhak asking these questions and looking for confirmation about the sin of foolish "games" and "practical jokes"; but when we consider the creative dialogues he would later have with God, it is hard to imagine that he himself did not possess a lively sense of humor. Thus, I hear in this question a young man concerned about his own natural tendencies to laughter (in the face of the stern and ascetic *kabbalah* he had studied prior to coming to Mezritch). This makes the answer of the Maggid all the more wonderful, as he is similtaneously able to validate a young Ḥasid in his own natural disposition, while at the same time, elevating him through this teaching.

The sense of joy and fun that must have reigned in Mezritch, especially among the younger disciples, is something left out of many Hasidic tales (probably because these stories were not considered especially edifying). But joy is foundational to Hasidism, and the fun of the Hasidic celebratory gathering *(farbrengen)* is a mainstay of Hasidic life. Even among the very 'serious' ḤaBaD-Lubavitcher Ḥasidim, we had fun; and this is true of the other Ḥasidim with whom I have celebrated in New York and Israel.

Indeed, it was likely this sense of fun that first led early Ḥasidim into clashes with the opponents of Hasidism in Lithuania, where the Ḥasidim of Ahron of Karlin and Avraham of Kalisk were known to turn cartwheels in the streets! This raucous behavior soon led to criticism from the authorities, and even the Maggid reprimanded them for going too far.

Divine Games

This backlash from society may be one reason we do not have more of the joy of Hasidic gatherings preserved in the literature; but before we stray too far, let us return to Reb Levi Yitzhak's dialogue with the Maggid.

I then raised another question: "When a father reduces and compresses *(m'tzamtzem)* his thought into the 'smallness' needed to communicate with his child, surely this is not the truth?"

He answered: "'And God *descended* on Mount Sinai.' (Exod. 19:18) But was it not so from the beginning, for there is no space empty of God?[2] Is not the whole world filled by God's glory? (Isa. 6:3) What is meant by 'descended' is that, in order for God to manifest in the world of feeling and experience, God needed to 'descend' to *our level* of experience."

It seems to me that this is the truth, that God's truth was disclosed in all the worlds.[3]

So Reb Levi Yitzhak ends with this resolution, "God's truth was disclosed in all the worlds," meaning, that there is truth even in jokes, games and pretending, just as there is in the scaling down of knowledge for particular ears.[4] It is interesting that

A Merciful God

Reb Levi Yitzhak even brings the Maggid's favorite analogy of the parent and child back to him as part of his own question, as if he was not certain that he had really understood what the Maggid had meant, saying, "Surely this is not the truth?"[5]

Later, Reb Levi Yitzhak would write of jokes in his own work, *Kedushat Levi*, while discussing the mysterious animals called *taḥash* in Torah . . .

Occasionally, someone tells a joke, while on the inside remaining attached to the fear of God. This is similar to the fur of the *tahash* used on the outer part of the Sanctuary, while the inside was full of the fear of God. Therefore, it is clear that the joke, like the outer part of the Sanctuary, is only a cover for that fear, and may allow one to receive the inner part.[6]

A Hasid for a Son-in-Law

As far as his father-in-law could tell, the decision to allow Reb Levi Yitzhak to study with the Ḥasidim was having no good results. He had thought he was bringing home one of the most promising minds of his generation and he had gotten a 'Ḥasid' instead.

Until Reb Levi Yitzhak began to frequent the *tish* of the Maggid of Mezritch, he was much admired for his talents, and considered a particularly fine feather in the cap of his father-in-law in Libertov. But soon after his visits to Mezritch began, so did the talk that Yisra'el Peretz' brilliant young son-in-law was becoming a 'good-for-nothing' Hasid. But as Peretz was still among the most prominent members of the community, the community continued to honor him, asking his son-in-law, Levi Yitzhak, to recite the passage *Attah ha-Reita*—"Unto you it was shown . . ." (Deut. 4:35)[1]—before the congregation on Simhat Torah.

Thus, Reb Levi Yitzhak ascended the *bimah* to recite the passage. But, even as he did so, he appeared absorbed in thought, and so long did he stand in silence on the *bimah* that the congregation started to squirm in their seats. Finally, to everyone's relief, he reached for his *tallit* to begin; but he immediately laid it down again, continuing his silent absorption. The congregation began to murmur. Worse still, the heads of the community began to whisper at his much embarrassed father-in-law to urge him to begin. Soon, his father-in-law called a servant to deliver a terse message to Reb Levi Yitzhak.

After the message had been delivered, Reb Levi Yitzhak said aloud, "Alright!" He then reached for his *tallit* once more. But even as it brushed his shoulders, he quickly drew it off again! His father-in-law reddened with shame and anger, burying his head in his hands.

Just then, Reb Levi Yitzhak's voice broke through the uncomfortable silence—*"If you know the words, and you are such a Hasid, then you recite it!"* He then left the *bimah* and returned to his place among the congregation, who watched in stunned silence.

His father-in-law seethed, but said nothing.

After they had gone home, Reb Levi Yitzhak sat at the dinner table eating happily, as if nothing had happened. But his father-in-law was unable to contain himself any longer and lashed out—*"What were you doing up there? Why have you brought this disgrace on me?!"*

A Hasid for a Son-in-Law

Reb Levi Yitzhak gazed at his father-in-law with sudden understanding. He now recognized how his behavior must have seemed and began to explain . . .

"My honored father-in-law, I am so sorry; I didn't mean to embarrass you! When I reached for my *tallit* in the beginning to recite the passage, my *yetzer ha-ra* (evil inclination) suddenly whispered in my ear, 'Why don't *I* recite the passage with you!'

"I asked, 'Who are you that you should think yourself worthy of such an honor?'

"The *yetzer ha-ra* replied, 'And who are *you* that you think yourself worthy of this honor?'

"I said proudly, 'I know the passage and its meanings.'

"But it merely replied, 'And so do I.'

"I asked, 'Where did you study?'

"'Where did you study?' it shot back.

"I told it that I had studied 'with my honored father, then in Yaroslav, then with the great Rabbi Shmelke Horowitz in Ritchovol, and now with the light of our generation, Rabbi Dov Baer, the Maggid of Mezritch!'

"Thinking that this would end the annoying dialogue—at the very point your message reached me—I reached for my *tallit* again.

A Merciful God

"Then the *yetzer ha-ra* said slyly, 'And I was with you in Husakov, in Yaroslav, in Ritchovol . . . *and* in Mezritch!'

This last comment stunned me so much that I put my *tallit* down again, protesting, 'I am a Hasid of the Maggid of Mezritch!'

"'And so am I,' said the *yetzer ha-ra*. 'I became one at the same time you did, and now I want to recite the *Attah ha-Reita* with you!'

"But now I knew my enemy, and I'd had enough. I said aloud, *'If you know the words, and you are such a Hasid, then you recite it!'* and I left him to recite the passage."[2]

The realization that the *yetzer ha-ra* accompanies us everywhere—stowing itself away in our subconscious motives—is among the most important realizations a Ḥasid must face.

In this story, Reb Levi Yitzhak handles it in the only way a Ḥasid can, *by sacrifice.* He sacrificed his own honor in the face of the congregation to serve God in purity, giving up his hidden motives in a single moment, without explanation. But as he recognized that his father-in-law had been shamed by this, and may have even thought that the last comment was aimed at him, Reb Levi Yitzhak felt it necessary to explain the truth to him.

A Hasid for a Son-in-Law

On another occasion, his father-in-law said to him, "Levi Yitzhak, I am prepared to forgive all of this foolishness, if you will only tell me what you have learned with this Maggid that is so special."

Reb Levi Yitzhak replied after a moment, "That there is a God in heaven who created the world."

His father-in-law scoffed and said, "Who doesn't know that?"

He then called for the maid and asked her, "Do you know who created the world?"

"God in heaven!" she replied, surprised at being asked such a question.

But Reb Levi Yitzhak said, "Yes, anyone can say this; but only one who has learned from the mouth of the great Maggid can know it *(Zi redt un ich vayss)!*"[3]

Splendor of the Face

The following account illustrates precisely what Reb Levi Yitzhak was trying to get across to his father-in-law. Here he tells us of a significant encounter with the Maggid in which no words were spoken, but much was communicated.

One year, the holiday of Rosh ha-Shanah fell on Shabbat, when it is forbidden to blow the *shofar* announcing the New Year.

On the second day of Rosh ha-Shanah, when it is permitted, the time came for the blowing of the *shofar*, but the Maggid was not well enough to blow it himself, so someone else did it in his place.

When Minhah arrived, my teacher arose to pray with us, and his words were like a holy fire! It was always like this with him at Minhah.

When I saw this, I went to stand and pray near the window where my teacher always prayed.

After he had completed the Amidah, he would pace back and forth for a few moments and go over to the window. At that moment, he slowly turned away from the window and suddenly I beheld his face. It was lit with glory and a scintillating spectrum of heavenly light!

A holy awe fell upon me and I stumbled backward, reaching for support. I was then caught by friends, who could not understand the reason for my stumbling.

My teacher noticed this and turned his face to the wall, resting his head there for several minutes. When he looked up again, there was no trace of the former splendor.

I never saw such splendor again until the time of my master's passing. Yet, it was from the splendor and majesty that shone upon his face that I was able to understand his Torah.[1]

Reb Levi Yitzhak's friend and fellow disciple, Reb Shneur Zalman of Liadi, was said to be deeply fond of the verse, "wisdom makes the face shine" (Eccles. 8:1), and one can certainly understand why if he had ever himself seen the Maggid's face in this state.

This transformative moment reminds us of the moment when the Maggid himself experienced the *mamash* (palpable) quality of the lights and angelic beings in the Ba'al Shem Tov's presence, bringing the words of Torah to life.[2] Similarly, the Berditchever tells us, "Yet, it was from that splendor and majesty that shone upon his face that I was able to understand his Torah," just as it had been for the Maggid.

The Troubles
of a Tzaddik

After a while, the financial fortunes of his father-in-law changed drastically and Reb Levi Yitzhak set out on the road to gather money for his recovery. He obtained a post as rabbi in Ritchovol, a position lately abandoned by his teacher and friend, Reb Shmelke of Nikolsburg. But he was soon forced to leave Ritchovol because of anti-Hasidic pressures from the Mitnaggedim, fleeing on the holiday of Sukkot with *lulav* and *etrog* still in hand!

Another post in Zhelikoff went better, and Reb Levi Yitzhak made many positive changes in the community; but he was eventually forced to leave Zhelikoff as well. Worst of all was his terrible treatment in Pinsk, where he was again run out of town, this time with the support of the famed Ga'on of Vilna. It was only after he settled in Berditchev that he at last found a peaceful home.

The holy Ba'al Shem Tov had this to say to his disciples on the day Reb Levi Yitzhak was born . . . "Today, a holy soul has entered the world, a soul who will stand up and defend all of Yisra'el.

A Merciful God

I tell you, this event has caused an uproar in the Heavenly Assembly, as Satan was terribly shaken by this news and came to complain before the Throne, saying . . .

> 'I am aware of a new soul in the world who will be a kind and fierce defender of the people. I can see that he will also be a great Torah scholar. His prayer will be like that of Rabbi Akiva, who never completed his *davvenen* (prayer) in the same corner he began. *Ribbono shel Olam* (Master of the Universe), this soul will cleanse the hearts of an entire generation and all my labors will be in vain!'

"The blessed and holy one answered Satan, 'Do not upset yourself; this soul will not have much time to cleanse hearts; after all, he will be a rabbi in Yisra'el.'"[1]

There is something so true in this anecdote. It is hard to think of any rebbe whose commitment to compassionate action and social justice was as complete as Reb Levi Yitzhak's; and yet, few if any of the disciples of the Maggid of Mezritch encountered as much resistance and persecution as he in his early

The Troubles of a Tzaddik

years. In one famous prayer, Reb Levi Yitzhak says, *"Ribbono shel Olam,* I do not ask that you reveal the secrets of your ways—I could not comprehend them. I do not ask why it is that I suffer, only tell me, do I suffer for your sake?"

Levi Yitzhak, 'the Merciful'

Like the holy Ba'al Shem Tov, Reb Levi Yitzhak also had a government issued last name. In that time, very few Jews had surnames, being known mostly by their own and their parent's names (for instance, Yisra'el ben Eliezer and Levi Yitzhak ben Meir). So when the civil authorities came around and required a surname for public records, most were forced to come up with a name quickly. When the Ba'al Shem Tov was asked his last name, he responded, "Tallismacher," explaining to his disciples later, "After all, what do I do but make a *tallit* (prayer shawl) for all Yisra'el."

One day, a public official knocked at the door of Reb Levi Yitzhak's home and made him aware of the king's decree that everyone in the realm must have a last name. Then he shot out a question that sounded more like a command, "Last name?!" Reb Levi Yitzhak looked heavenward and said *"Derbaramdiger*—O 'merciful' God—what kind of name should I have?! How should I be known in this world?! Is it not said, 'As God is merciful, so shall you be merciful'?" (Shabbat 113b)[1]

But even as Reb Levi Yitzhak continued his dialogue with God, the official simply took out his notebook and wrote down the first word Reb Levi Yitzhak had uttered, "Derbaramdiger," or 'merciful,' and promptly left the house.[2]

Of course no name could be more suitable than 'merciful' for such a soul as Reb Levi Yitzhak. We are taught that when Adam named all of God's creatures in the beginning, he did not name them randomly, but rather according to their essence; for the name and the essence were one.

Head and Heels

Now we will begin to look at the Torah of Reb Levi Yitzhak of Berditchev, which was truly in harmony with his own life and service to God. This is true of most of the Hasidic rebbes, but it seems especially true with Reb Levi Yitzhak; for the sacred anecdotes that are told of his life seem like practical illustrations of what he advocates in his teaching. The teachings were more sophisticated, of course, but almost always put a compassionate frame around God's creation (especially as regards human beings). These teachings are primarily drawn from his book *Kedushat Levi*, originally published in Slavita in 1788.

There is a person who serves the blessed creator and becomes aware of the divine oneness through digging deeply with the mind, coming to an understanding of God's undivided divinity through mental rigor. But there is another person who serves the blessed creator and understands the divine oneness through active faith in the reality of God, who creates all things, and does not spend any time digging with reason. *Ha-klal*[1]—therefore,

25

deriving from the general rule—just as a person has a head, a torso and heels, so too is divine service accomplished with the head, the torso and the heels.

The 'head' is the service of one who digs with the mind, and comes to understand that there is indeed a God in the world, and that God is truly one.

The 'heels' refer to the service of faith, because it is on the ground level, at the end of the rungs.

But what is the service of the 'torso' then? This is connected to the 'arms' of the torso that point to the love of the creator and indicate from whence the love is derived. Sometimes they reach up to the head, which means that the love one has for the creator is influenced by the mind. While at other times the arms are below, meaning that the love of God comes from simple faith. So the arms may point to a love and understanding of the divine oneness and the goodness of God coming from the 'head' or the 'heels.' But if one really wishes to be in palpable contact with the oneness of God, serving in the most desirable way, one should do it through an active faith.[2]

This is a teaching that shows us the difference between what are sometimes spoken of as

Head and Heels

ḤaGaT and ḤaBaD Hasidism. *ḤaBaD* stands for *ḥokhmah* (wisdom), *binah* (understanding), and *da'at* (knowledge); in other words, the upper *sefirot* or divine attributes dealing with mentation. Whereas *ḤaGaT* stands for *ḥesed* (loving-kindness), *gevurah* (strength), and *tiferet* (beauty), the emotional attributes of divinity.

ḤaBaD Hasidism asks the question, 'What do you do when you are not feeling particularly connected to God? Or worse, when you are under a malaise, feeling dull in the head and heart?' The emotion of love is simply not available and needs to be awakened. This can be accomplished by using the mind (in profound contemplation) until it begins to stir the dormant feelings in the heart. This approach is almost exclusively associated with Reb Levi Yitzhak's close friend, Reb Shneur Zalman of Liadi and his heirs, who identify themselves as ḤaBaD Ḥasidim. However, there are other Hasidic rebbes who could also be said to emphasize a ḤaBaD-type approach that is not based on the system of Reb Shneur Zalman, for it is really a matter of temperament and the need of the specific individual.[3]

Nevertheless, Reb Levi Yitzhak of Berditchev says, while both of these approaches exist and are necessary—as he must have seen in Mezritch—the way of ḤaGaT Hasidism and simple faith is preferable to the digging of the mind.[4] This is what the "arms" in his teaching tell us; for the arms in their natural resting state, as well as in most activities, are usually below the head. It is only in the extraordinary situation that we put them above the head, because of the great effort involved in this action.

His friend, Reb Shneur Zalman does not disagree, but finds that a faith unconsidered with the mind, and unable or unwilling to struggle with ideas, tends to be a weak faith. But Reb Shneur Zalman was a 'Litvak,' serving the intellectuals of Lithuania who prized knowledge above all. So not only was this approach (of first going through the mind) natural to him (as perhaps the most intellectual of all the Maggid's disciples), it was necessary for opening the hearts of the intellectuals whom he served. Reb Levi Yitzhak, on the other hand, was the genius (as we said before) who was ready to trade his intellect for love and purity, and served a congregation that was much less rigorous about intellectual achievement. Thus he favored the approach of simple faith.

The Darkened Shell

So how did Reb Levi Yitzhak break the shell over the hardened hearts of his disciples, if not with the mind, as was necessary for Reb Shneur Zalman and the heady Lithuanians? Because of the great love and friendship between Reb Shneur Zalman and Reb Levi Yitzhak, there are many tales of the Berditchever preserved in the ḤaBaD-Lubavitch oral tradition. This one, usually called 'the Shvartze *K'lippah'* (the black shell, or demon) among ḤaBaD Hasidim, was told by my *rebbe* Yosef Yitzhak of Lubavitch of blessed memory . . .

Early one morning, Reb Levi Yitzhak of Berditchev called three of his close disciples and said "Prepare for a journey." Shortly thereafter, they climbed into the carriage and were off. They traveled fast (faster than the disciples liked), but no one dared to say anything or even to ask where they were going, as it was clear that the *rebbe* had some definite purpose in mind. During the journey, he only permitted them one short stop to say *t'hillim* (Psalms) before setting out again at the same pace.

A Merciful God

Finally, as evening approached, the carriage slowed to a stop in front of a house near a great estate. The house obviously belonged to the estate's land agent, and from within the carriage they could hear the bark of a large dog. Now it turned out that the land agent was a notorious Jew-hater and had trained his enormous black dog to attack Jews on command. Alerted by the dog's barking, the land agent looked out of his window and saw by their dress that it was a carriage full of Jews. He immediately opened the door of the house to let his dog out to harass them and emerged just after carrying a loaded pistol!

He was a fierce looking man with murderous rage in his eyes. Reb Levi Yizhak's disciples were terrified. After all, there was no law that was going to prevent him from murdering them right then and there. Over the barking and growls of the black dog, they heard the man yelling, "Get off of my property before I put a shot through your head!"

Reb Levi Yitzhak seemed unperturbed and leaned out of the window with his calm face shining and said, "Sir, we are Jews on a journey and only wish to stop for our evening prayers." As the disciples expected, this sent the land agent into a fury and he pointed the pistol at Reb Levi Yitzhak's calm face and fired! . . . *Only, the gun didn't fire* . . . There was only the snap of the hammer making contact. The land agent looked at the pistol curiously—turning it sideways as if to ask it what had happened—when all of a sudden it went off! To his horror, he found that he had killed his own dog!

Reb Levi Yitzhak told one of his disciples to exit the carriage now and repeat his request to the land agent. With trepidation, the disciple got down and walked over to the agent and stammered, "Sir, we are Hasidim traveling with the holy Rabbi Levi Yitzhak of Berditchev; it is time for our evening prayers and we would like to ask your kind permission to pray in your house."

The land agent looked stunned, staring absently in the direction of his beloved dog. He mouthed the words, "The Rabbi of Berditchev" slowly. A distant echo of recognition entered his mind, "The famous holy man of Berditchev." Still staring past the disciple, he managed to say as if in a dream, "You have my permission; please come into the house."

The man turned to walk back toward his house, as the disciple walked back to the carriage cautiously (not wanting to turn his back on the man) to convey the land agent's unexpected consent to the *rebbe*. The disciples were perplexed by this turn of events, perhaps even more so than they had been by the journey and the threat of violence. The land agent was no less confused; after all, he pistol was clean and in good order. What had happened? Could it have been the power of this holy man?

A Merciful God

The news that the famed Rabbi of Berditchev was going to say his evening prayers at the house of the land agent traveled fast, and curiosity quickly overcame the local Jews' fear of the land agent. Obviously, something extraordinary was happening. Soon there was a large gathering at the house to pray with Reb Levi Yitzhak, and the land agent merely sat back in confused silence at the strange scene unfolding in his home.

Then Reb Levi Yitzhak began the evening prayers with *Shir ha-Ma'alot.* But when he reached the words, "Merciful One, forgive our sins, and do not arouse your anger" (Ps. 78:38), the *rebbe* stopped and began to sing a haunting *niggun* that moved everyone who listened to it . . ."

Somehow, the *niggun*—though itself wordless—communicated a message to each and every person present. It seemed to begin with a tragic statement about life, as if saying . . . 'Yes, life takes us all into dark places. How could we be happy about that? But this is how it is; there must be a deeper reason.' Then, as the *niggun* continued, it began to describe the regret and folly of our lives, seeming to say, 'But this is not who we wanted to be.' Then a growing hope began to build in its ascending phrases, until finally the *rebbe* lifted his arms to heaven and the melody reached a crescendo of poignant joy and pain all at once! Everyone was transported to the purifying 'waters above.' If only they could have lingered there! But the *niggun* was

The Darkened Shell

already descending with a sigh, gently rocking them back to the earth, comforted, and yet still longing for the regions of forgiveness and healing they were permitted to taste. Finally, the *niggun* receded into silence before Reb Levi Yitzhak called out, "O God, save us! O Sovereign, answer us on the day we call out to you!" (Ps. 20:10)

At that very moment, the land agent, who had been completely absorbed in the melody, fell down in a faint and was carried to a quiet corner of the house.

After the prayers were over, the land agent asked to speak with Reb Levi Yitzhak in private. He told him, "I was born in Germany to Jewish parents; but when I was a young man, I joined the Kaiser's army. The higher I rose in rank, the looser my ties to Judaism became; for the more I was held in awe by the soldiers under me, the less awe I felt for God. By the time I was appointed to be a personal guard of the Kaiser, I was no longer even a Jew. Worse still, I had learned to despise Jews and to persecute them, and this I have done until this very day."

These last words he uttered with reddened eyes and a tear-streaked face. What the *rebbe* said to him then remains a secret.

When he came out from his meeting with the *rebbe*, he walked over to the disciples and took their hands warmly, saying a long unused, *"Shalom aleikhem*—I too am a Jew," and he told them his story and begged their forgiveness. He then borrowed a *tallit* and *t'fillin* and they helped to reacquaint him with the prayers.

When Reb Levi Yitzhak and his disciples got back into the carriage, the *rebbe* warned his disciples not to speak about this journey to anyone. A short time later, the land agent quit the estate and sold all his possessions. No one in that area ever heard from him again. But around the same time, a stranger came to live and study in Berditchev, becoming a close disciple of Reb Levi Yitzhak and the founder of a prominent Jewish family in Berditchev.[1]

Reb Levi Yitzhak had reached into the very heart of compassion, gently cleansing the land agent's soul of all the accretions of pride and anger, pain and regret, until it was finally ready to embrace God once again in love *(ahavah)* and awe *(yirah)*.

Whole-Hearted Prayer

This brings us to Reb Levi Yitzhak's prayer. As we saw in the preceding story, prayer can be as transformative for the one praying as for those who tune-in to the frequency of that prayer. This is what Reb Avraham Yehoshua Heschel of Apt meant when he said, "Prayer can only be learned from a praying person."

You should always pray with an enflamed fervor; but today, because of our sins, we have small minds, and cannot begin our prayers with that great fervor. Thus, it is only after we have been praying for a while that our words begin to take on a life of their own. But when the *Mashiah* (Messiah) comes, "The world will be filled with knowledge as the waters cover the sea," (Hab. 2:14), and we will begin our prayers with that great fervor.[1]

Thus, Reb Levi Yitzhak introduces us to the quality of prayer that is desirable. The problem is, that quality is not easily accessible because of the smallness of our minds. What does this mean? Consider what is written in the *Sh'ma* . . .

> Be aware . . . watch out! Don't let your cravings delude you. Don't become alienated by them. Don't let your cravings become your gods. Don't debase yourself before them, because the God-sense within you will become distorted, heaven will be shut to you, and grace will not descend." (Deut. 13:16-17)[2]

We can see from this that the greater mind is the one into which the God-sense is flowing freely and where it is not distorted; and it is this is the mind that would allow us to pray with "an enflamed fervor" right from the beginning.

In another important passage, Reb Levi Yitzhak goes on to speak about what we should do in our prayer . . .

Your prayer can be considered 'good' when you sing praises to your creator with your entire heart. That is to say, while cleaving (*d'veikut*) to God with a holy awe (*yirah*), abandoning all extraneous thoughts (*mahshavot zarot*), and constellating all of your intention (*kavvanah*) around the giving of joy to your maker, arousing and putting all the energy of your body, speech and mind into that one service, until even your bones are praying!

You should find every opportunity to say to God, 'How compassionate you are my God! How good and kind you are to me!' For when you do so, it is impossible not to be touched by these same attributes. That is to say, because your focus and energy are flowing into these attributes *(middot)* of kindness and compassion, they are catalyzed in you, causing you to be, for instance, good to others and kind to the poor.

Therefore, choose your own ideals of virtue and praise God with them. Then you will not forsake those virtues in your own life; in the moment of fervor and concentration, when you are attributing these virtues *(middot)* to God, you are attuning to their divine archetypes, which releases their light and beauty into your being. Thus you are bound by mighty bonds of love to the creator, and to the positive attributes of compassion, gentleness, and kindness. In this state, if you ask something of God, then how could you not get a good answer?[3]

After hearing this holy Torah, it only seems appropriate to say *"ha-klal"*—Reb Levi Yitzhak's chosen phrase for framing his point—because this seems to be the summary of all his teaching and all the stories that are told about him. First he deals with the preliminaries of prayer in which one invests one's entire being—engaging both a numinous sense of the *mysterium fascinans* (compelling mystery) and the *mysterium tremendum* (trembling mystery)—getting all the fibers of one's being to vibrate with the desire to give pleasure to God, to take God into the place of feeling good. Then one begins to praise God with all of those attributes one most admires, and most desires to see activated in one's own life. For this is how Reb Levi Yitzhak deals with the notion of "The *tzaddik* decrees and the holy one fulfills."[4] For through this kind of fervor and energy in prayer, we can open a connection between the divine and the human. Through this we may stimulate a response from God above, which in turn, touches us here below. It is an open connection going both ways . . . *the one who touches is touched.*[5] We become what we seek. Clearly, Reb Levi Yitzhak took seriously the words in Torah that say, "Be you holy as I am holy." (Lev. 11:44)

The Parable
of the King's Joy

As a good spiritual director, Reb Levi Yitzhak also dealt with the subtle issues of temptation and how one can become sidetracked and even fall into sin during moments of spiritual joy and exultation, as we see in the following parable . . .

Once upon a time, the son of the king who had long been at war with the king's enemies finally returned home victorious. His father, the king, was very proud of his son. He decided to host a celebration in his son's honor. At the celebration, the king was in such a good mood that he decided to grant any wish asked of him! For that is the way of the king—when he is in his joy, he fulfills all that he is asked to fulfill.

In the middle of the celebration, the king's enemy entered the court, hoping to take advantage of the king's joy. Now, if the king forgets to look at the root of his joy, he will certainly fulfill the request of the enemy. But if the king remembers to look at the root of his joy, he will recognize that the enemy's request is in conflict with his joy (derived from his son's victory over this same enemy), and will ignore it.

Therefore, it is written, "I am my beloved's and my beloved's desire is for me." (Songs 7:11) For it is known that Yisra'el arose in the mind of the divine, and it is because of the souls of Yisra'el that the world was created. Thus, when Yisra'el is doing what God asks, God is delighted and given great joy, sending all good things into the world because of Yisra'el. But God makes certain that this good is directed and channeled to the proper places, because there are external and evil forces that would also like to receive the flow of God's generosity. Therefore, it is important for God to examine the root of the intent, so that no part of the flow of divine generosity should be diverted into unworthy places.[1]

There is an energy that comes with joy and exultation; it is a 'Yes! energy' and seeks to accommodate everything that comes its way. But consider how when one's energy is 'up,' and one's heart and mind are wide open, how often one is also open to baser thoughts and desires. The energy

The Parable of the King's Joy

simply wants to flow, but we need to be skillful about where it gets directed at these times. For, as Reb Levi Yitzhak teaches, the spiritual benefit of the energy-flow will not follow as the energy gets directed into unworthy places. Therefore, we must be vigilant at all times.

Spiritual Audacity

One day, my wife Eve, a talented practitioner of guided imagery exercises, took me on an imaginal journey that ended up at the grave of Reb Levi Yitzhak of Berditchev. Actually, she did not take me there, but that is nevertheless where I ended up. I recognized it because I had been there before on a pilgrimage to the graves of the rebbes in 2005.

As I entered the *ohel*—the building enclosing the graves—in my imagination, the cover lifted from the grave and Reb Levi Yitzhak emerged from within. He seemed tall and his eyes were kind. He bid me welcome with a *Shalom aleikhem* and I took the opportunity to ask him a question . . . "How might I connect to the same *kavvanah* (intention) and *d'veikut* (adherence to God) you must have felt as you sang your famous song, 'To the East is You; to the West is You . . .' ?" Basically, I was asking him how I could encounter the divine presence in a palpable way. Then Reb Levi Yitzhak replied, V*art nisht oif kine kovved*, "Don't wait for an invitation," which meant, don't wait around for it to happen, or even until you have committed yourself to the presence—just move ahead. Reb Levi Yitzhak was the humblest of men, but in his service to God, his motto was to be bold!

A Merciful God

One has to recognize just how precious one's service is to God. A person must in many ways be humble in all that one does; but if someone were to tell me that I should also be humble in the service of God . . . *God forbid it!* On the contrary, a person has to say, "The acts that I am doing, fulfilling the *mitzvot*, are so precious to our blessed creator, who takes such delight in them! If I were to be humble about them, saying, 'Of what worth is my service to God?' that would be nothing less than heresy!"[1]

There is a sense in which the world stands on this activity—on my next *mitzvah*, on the next word of my prayer—and that is what Reb Levi Yitzhak is getting into here.

I am reminded of an encounter that the Swiss psychologist Carl Jung (1875-1961) had with a Native American elder called 'Mountain Lake' in New Mexico. I find it so relevant to this discussion that I would like to quote it in full and leave it to you to ponder . . .

"What we do, we do not only for ourselves but . . . for the whole world. Everyone benefits by it."

Spiritual Audacity

I could observe from his excitement that he was alluding to some extremely important element of his religion. I therefore asked him: "You think, then, that what you do in your religion benefits the whole world?" He replied with great animation, "Of course. If we did not do it, what would become of the world?" And with a significant gesture he pointed to the sun. . . . "After all," he said, "we are a people who live on the roof of the world; we are the sons of Father Sun, and with our religion we daily help our father to go across the sky. We do this not only for ourselves, but for the whole world. If we were to cease practicing our religion, in ten years the sun would no longer rise. Then it would be night forever."

I then realized on what the "dignity," the tranquil composure of the individual Indian, was founded. It springs from his being a son of the sun; his life is cosmologically meaningful, for he helps the father and preserver of all life in his daily rise and descent. If we set against this our own self-justifications, the meaning of our own lives as it is formulated by our reason, we cannot help but see our poverty. Out of sheer envy we are obliged to smile at the Indians' naivete and to plume ourselves on our cleverness; for otherwise we would discover how impoverished and down at the heels we are. Knowledge does not enrich us; it removes us more and more from the mythic world in which we were once at home by right of birth.

If for a moment we put away all European rationalism and transport ourselves into the clear mountain air of that solitary plateau, which drops off on one side into the broad continental prairies and on the other into the Pacific Ocean; if we also set aside our intimate knowledge of the world and exchange it for a horizon that seems immeasurable, and an ignorance of what lies beyond it, we will begin to achieve an inner comprehension of the Pueblo Indian's point of view. "All life comes from the mountain" is immediately convincing to him, and he is equally certain that he lives upon the roof of an immeasurable world, closest to God. He above all others has the Divinity's ear, and his ritual act will reach the distant sun soonest of all. [. . .]

The ritual acts of man are an answer and reaction to the action of God upon man; and perhaps they are not only that, but are also intended to be "activating," a form of magic coercion. That man feels capable of formulating valid replies to the over-powering influence of God, and that he can render back some thing which is essential even to God, induces pride, for it raises the human individual to the dignity of a metaphysical factor. "God and us"— even if it is only an unconscious sous-entendu [Fr., implied, understood by innuendo]—this equation no doubt underlies that enviable serenity of the Pueblo Indian. Such a man is in the fullest sense of the word in his proper place.[2]

The Advocate

As we have seen, the weight of human significance underlies every story and teaching of Reb Levi Yitzhak, especially those in which he acts as an advocate for the people with God, arguing for divine justice in the tradition of Abraham. The following story (a favorite of mine) illustrates this advocacy perfectly . . .

One Pesah, Reb Levi Yitzhak of Berditchev called two of his *gabbaim* (attendants), Leibel the Yellow and Leibel the Black, and said, "I cannot begin the Passover *seder* until I have two things." To Leibel the Yellow he said, "Go from house to house and bring me back as much smuggled Turkish tobacco as you can find." To Leibel the Black he said, "Go out and find me a little *hametz*, a little leavened bread that I can use for a healing." The *gabbaim* were astonished by these requests, but nevertheless, went out in search of tobacco and *hametz* to bring to the *rebbe*.

After several hours, the first *gabbai* returns with two helpers carrying a load of Turkish tobacco.

A Merciful God

Shortly thereafter, the second *gabbai* returns empty-handed. Seeing this, Reb Levi Yitzhak turned his gaze to heaven and said, *"Ribbono shel Olam*, do you see? The Czar has his soldiers posted every 100 yards with orders to 'shoot-to-kill' to prevent the smuggling of Turkish tobacco along the border; but you have no soldiers, and have asked us not to have any *hametz* in our homes over Pesah, and you see there is none! Beloved creator, perhaps it is time you relieved our misery and set us free from this Egypt!"

Then he began the *seder*.

For Reb Levi Yitzhak, this was no mere game to entertain his Ḥasidim, but a holy case he could bring before the court of the Heavenly Assembly, the tobacco and *hametz* his evidence. "Justice, Justice you shall pursue" (Deut. 16:20), even with God. He did not do this in anger against God, but to bring down mercy for the people. God's wisdom is perfect, but the appearance of things in the world does not seem at all perfect to us. What can we do? Someone must be an advocate for the people. Should we not also seek justice for the way things *seem* to us? In his *Kedushat Levi*, Reb Levi Yitzhak goes on to tell us that this kind of advocacy is a prerequisite for leaders in Yisra'el . . .

The Advocate

"May the Lord appoint a leader over Yisra'el."[1]

Ha-klal—therefore, deriving from the general rule—one can always manage to find merit in the people of Yisra'el, even if they are not doing the will of God like angels; after all, they are so busy making a living. This was the way of Avraham, our father, as well; for he was a person of *hesed* (loving-kindness) and always finding ways to say something good about his children. This is why he served food to the angels, so that they would realize that human beings need to eat!

So how should God appoint a leader over Yisra'el? By choosing one who can lead the children of Yisra'el in the same way as God acts with regard to Yisra'el. Thus, we can always say to God, "Why did you make it so that we could sin? After all, you could have made us without sin! Therefore, you are an accessory to our crimes and have to forgive us!"[2]

One last anecdote to illustrate how Reb Levi Yitzhak put this teaching into practice himself, showing himself to be a true "leader over Yisra'el," always finding some point of goodness in the lives of simple Jews who were so "busy making a living" . . .

A Merciful God

One day, Reb Levi Yitzhak of Berditchev is walking down the street when he notices an old Yiddeleh (Jew) greasing the wheels of his wagon while wearing his *tallit* and *t'fillin*, hurriedly mumbling his prayers! At that moment, a passerby sees the same sight and cries out, *"Shaygetz!* What are you doing greasing your wheels in *tallit* and *t'fillin*!"* But Reb Levi Yitzhak looked heavenward in the sight of both men and cried aloud, *"Oy! Ribbono shel Olam*—what remarkable servants you have! Even when they're greasing the wheels of their wagons they can't take their minds off of you!"[3]

The Small Siddur

While the stories of Reb Levi Yitzhak's great compassion and 'spiritual audacity' are no doubt true, there is a danger that they might also overwhelm our awareness of his 'human-ness,' presenting us with an idealized caricature instead of a man. But Reb Levi Yitzak was a man; and this is important to know, because we cannot follow in the footsteps of a caricatured ideal. Reb Levi Yitzhak was indeed extraordinary, *and also human*. It has been said that he sometimes suffered from depression and "fell from his elevated rung," praying from "a small *siddur*" in those periods.[1] One such period was after the early death of his beloved son, Meir.

Rabbi Meir (d. 1806) was a commited Ḥasid of his father, author of the work *Keter Torah*, which Reb Levi Yitzhak quotes in his *Kedushat Levi*. When he died, Reb Levi Yitzhak was hit hard and composed a song, as if a dialogue between himself and his son . . .

Meir'l, my son,
Do you know who you are?

A Merciful God

I am dust and ashes, my father.

Meir'l, my son,
>Do you know before whom you stand?

Before the sovereign of sovereigns, my father.

Meir'l, my son,
>What do you ask of God?

Children, life and sustenance, my father.

Meir'l, my son,
>What do you mean by "children"?

Children who study Torah, my father.

Meir'l, my son,
>What do you mean by "life"?

A life of praise to God, my father.

Meir'l, my son,
>What do you mean by "sustenance"?

*"You shall eat and be satisfied and bless
the Lord your God" (Joel 2:26), my father.*[2]

The Small Siddur

The "small *siddur*" mentioned in Yitzhak of Kamarna's account of Reb Levi Yitzhak's depression is a subtle Hasidic metaphor; for Reb Levi Yitzhak was known for his long empassioned prayers. That he could not pray them in these periods of sadness, either burdened by the weight of persecution from the opponents of Hasidism, or in the period of grief over the death of his son, says much about the actual depth of his grief and sadness.

In a period of profound grief in my own life, I remembered the "small *siddur*" of Reb Levi Yitzhak and wrote this poem called "the small siddur" . . .

after the death of his son
reb levi yitzhak they say
prayed from 'a small siddur'

he was known for his long prayers
taking his time to warm them up   slowly
to make a fire bold out of old dry wood

but in the year of his grief he could not
hold that dense book of profound gratitude
too heavy for so heavy a heart broken

perhaps he wound them up quickly that year
or maybe he didn't even pray   to the taking-god
giving in return only a small ungrateful siddur

A Merciful God

but i think he merely forgot his prayers
forgot how to pray for anything in the absence
of the one thing that made them worthwhile

lost in a lethean riverwash of sorrow
there were no prayers to be said   because
there was no reb levi yitzhak to say them

not as he had ever been or known himself to be
lost on a bark in that river known only
to the living who've known the death of a love
    the ones who make the silent prayer of the dead [3]

Thrice He Won

Justice was a major theme in the stories that Reb Levi Yitzhak told, and nowhere is this better illustrated than in this long *ma'aseh* (story) that he relates to his Ḥasidim. The brand of justice celebrated in this story is one that should inspire us all to purify our service to God.

It was the custom of Reb Levi Yitzhak of Berditchev to walk four paces with every Jew who was to be buried in his town—*not the whole way*—just the required four paces, and often a bit more. Nevertheless, when Reb Ya'akov the lumber merchant passed from this world, Reb Levi Yitzhak accompanied the body all the way to the gravesite.

When Reb Levi Yitzhak returned from the cemetery, he was in high spirits and his disciples were astonished, saying, "First he walks all the way to the grave and now he's in high spirits!" The *rebbe* called for food and invited his *talmidim* (disciples) to sit with him and eat, offering a *"L'hayyim!"* Then he began to speak, saying, "Ah! Reb Ya'akov was such a *tzaddik;* for he knew how to use the *beit din*, the court of law in the service of God. It is for this reason that I followed him to the place where his body would be returned to the earth. Why was Reb Ya'akov so special, you might ask? Because he won three *din* Torahs, three legal cases over which I presided! But the real question is, why was he at the *beit din* in the first place?"

Then Reb Levi Yitzhak began to describe the circumstances of the three lawsuits against Reb Ya'akov . . .

The First Din Torah

The first time I met Reb Ya'akov was at a *beit din* to which he had come with another man. It seems that Reb Ya'akov had been walking through the marketplace when his attention was drawn to a group of people huddled around a man who had just fainted. It turned out that the man's name was Shimon, a poor peddler who had a small store in an outlying village. Each year, Shimon made his way to Berditchev for the fair to make his purchases for the entire year. This time he had come with 300 rubles—150 of his own, and another 150 that he had borrowed.

When he had finished collecting his purchases, he went for his money and found that it was gone! *Stolen or lost?!* He suddenly felt ill and fainted. When he came to, he felt for his money once more and fainted again. Poor Shimon!

Thrice He Won

Reb Ya'akov watched the efforts of the people to revive him, and when he next opened his eyes, Reb Ya'akov said to him, "Reb Yid (Jew), I found your money, don't worry."

Shimon the peddler looked at him and fainted again—this time from relief.

When he came to, the bystanders gave him Reb Ya'akov's card asking Shimon to present himself at his home where he would have to establish his ownership before having his money refunded. The people followed Shimon to the house, but Reb Ya'akov admitted only Shimon.

"What was the money wrapped in?" asked Reb Ya'akov.

"A piece of red cotton," said Shimon, "the kind into which feathers are sewn to make a pillow."

"How large a piece of cotton was it?"

Shimon gave him the exact dimensions.

"What denominations of money were in there?"

Laboriously Shimon made his tally.

"Ten tens, twenty fives, twenty-five doubles, forty singles, and ten rubles in coin."

"Let me see if what I have matches your description."

He went into the next room, cut a pillow open and took a piece of red cotton the exact size, counted money into it according to the denominations Shimon had mentioned and brought this bundle of money to the peddler. He gave it to him and said, "It is yours. Go in peace."

While this was going on, another man came in, and as soon as Shimon left, he turned to Reb Ya'akov, saying, "Sir, what have you done to me? How could you give him back his money when I have it here in my pocket? I know, *because I stole it!* From the moment I heard that you had found the money, I knew that this deed had to be undone— Here, take the money back before it burns a hole in my pocket. Take your money!"

"Who are you?" Reb Ya'akov asked. "Do I know you? There is no agreement between us . . . I will not take your money."

"Then let us go to a *beit din*," the thief exclaimed, and the two appeared before me.

My decision was clear-cut. Reb Ya'akov was under no obligation to take the money. The thief was obliged to keep the money that he had acquired by illegal means. I am told that he gave some of the money for the dowry of a poor girl in the city, and the rest he distributed among the needy. When anyone offered him thanks, he responded, "It is not me you should thank."

The Second Din Torah

One day, Reb Ya'akov came in to see me with another man whom we'll just call 'Reuven.' Reuven had been a poor man at first, with little to feed his

Thrice He Won

wife and children. Deep in his heart he felt that his *mazel* (destiny) lay elsewhere, and that he needed to follow a path to a faraway place where he was sure to find the abundance heaven intended for him. In this way he could feed his family.

There was just one problem: every time he broached the subject with his wife, she refused to hear of it. "I don't want to move from here; we are known here, and the house of Yisra'el will deal kindly with us here. Whatever we have, let us have it together—whether a crust of bread or a bit of water."

But tell a bird not to fly! Reuven could not resist his intuition and the call of his *mazel,* and one day he came home with a *ma'aseh* (story) he had made up so that he could get away. He felt bad about the lies he was going to tell, but his *mazel* called!

"Give me a *mazel tov* (congratulations)!"

She was not in a particularly good mood that day and sneered *"Mazel tov"* back at him. Almost as an afterthought, she asked, "What for?"

"Because I have a job."

This changed everything, including her mood. "You have a job? *Mazel tov! Mazel tov!* With whom?"

"With Reb Ya'akov, the lumber merchant; he needs a manager in one of his forests to mark the trees for cutting, to see them tied into rafts so that they can be sent down the river to Danzig. I will have to work in the forest close by for days on end. But I have to go right away. Pack me some bread and some shirts while I fetch a few holy books, my *tallit* and *t'fillin*. I have to get off to work!"

"What about me?" she protested.

"Every Thursday morning you go to Reb Ya'akov's office and ask for seven rubles. That is the pay we agreed on. You will be well taken care of."

"Seven rubles—a king's dowry!" she exclaimed and went to fetch his things. Before she could even question him further as to the whereabouts of the forest, Reuven was off.

Thursday morning arrived, and Reuven's wife went to the office of Reb Ya'akov's bookkeeper and, almost giddy, asked for her husband's pay. But the bookkeeper didn't have any record of this fictitious deal between Reuven and Reb Ya'akov. He spoke gruffly to her, "Don't waste my time; I know of no new manager in any forest."

"Please read the list of your employees again; perhaps I mispronounced his name . . . Perhaps you have written it differently." She pleaded with him, fearful thoughts entering her head.

Seeing that she was not going to leave him alone, he started to read one name after another out loud. At the end, she fell into despair and accused the bookkeeper of withholding her husband's rightful salary.

She cried out, "Justice, mercy, *gevalt!*"

The door of the inner office opened and Reb Ya'akov came out to see what all the noise was about.

In tears, the woman repeated her story and a puzzled look came over Reb Ya'akov's face. Then, to his bookkeeper's shock, Reb Ya'akov said, "This is all my fault. I should have told you that I hired her husband. Please put her name on the books and make sure to pay her seven rubles per week and a bonus for the *Yamim Tovim,* the holy days"

The incredulous bookkeeper did as he was told, and the woman departed in joy.

Two and a half years went by in this way. Reuven did indeed find his *mazel,* and it turned out to be a *mazel tov!* So when he finally arrived home it was in a well-appointed carriage led by two horses. He was proud and happy to be coming home, and with such great success; but he was more anxious about what he would find and how he would be greeted. He stopped the carriage a ways off from the house and crept up to peep in the windows. There he saw his wife and children well-fed and nicely dressed with an air of well-being about them! He was pleased, but puzzled. Gathering his courage, he went to the door and knocked. To his eternal surprise, he was greeted with joy by his wife and children, and they all sat down to a good meal.

When Reuven questioned his wife as to how she had managed in his absence, she related that ever since the first Thursday when there was a little trouble, things had been going quite well for she had received his weekly wages from Reb Yaakov's bookkeeper.

Reuven was restless and could not sleep that night. Over and over, he tallied what he must owe to Reb Ya'akov; and in the morning, right after his prayers, he went to Reb Ya'akov with all the money that had been (in his mind) unwittingly 'loaned' to him.

"Reb Ya'akov," he said, "How can I thank you for what you have done for me? Nevertheless, I've come to repay you in full."

"Who are you?" Reb Ya'akov asked. "I have no agreement with you; I cannot take your money."

"Reb Ya'akov," Reuven pleaded, "I really needed it at the time; I had no choice. I apologize for what I did, but now I want to return the money that you gave to my poor wife."

"There is no loan agreement between us," Reb Ya'akov said flatly. "What was done was done for *HaShem* (God) and to help an abandoned wife. Your return and your wealth changes nothing."

Thrice He Won

In shame, Reuven begged him, "Please sir, I insist that I be allowed to pay you back for your kindness. If necessary, I will plead my case before the *beit din.*"

And so they came to stand before me. The decision was a simple one, as there was no word or agreement between them: the law could not force Reb Ya'akov to accept the money and lose the *mitzvah*. I told Reuven that he could do with his money as he saw fit, spend it on *mitzvot* if he wished. Then Reb Ya'akov and Reuven left as they had come in.

Since that time, Reuven has given generously to all in need. And when anyone tries to thank him, he responds cryptically, "It is not me you should thank." And if anyone tries to pay him back, he declares, "Only if the *beit din* requires that I accept."

The Third Din Torah

The last time Reb Ya'akov came before me was with Shlomo, a man of great wealth who had gotten into some financial trouble. It seems that Shlomo, in need of a large short-term loan, had approached Reb Ya'akov to lend him a thousand rubles for a month.

Reb Ya'akov asked, "Who will be your guarantor?"

A Merciful God

Hearing this, Shlomo was in a quandary. How could he involve another person in his debt? His credit and reputation would be ruined. Yet without the cash he would be bankrupt tomorrow. Bitterness welled-up in his heart and he pointed heavenward, saying, *"HaShem will be my guarantor!"*

"Fine," Reb Ya'akov said calmly, "who could have a better one?" He then counted out a thousand rubles to Shlomo's surprise and let him go.

When Shlomo returned to repay his loan, Reb Ya'akov simply said, "I'm sorry Shlomo, I cannot accept payment twice on the same loan; your Guarantor has already repaid me."

Shlomo could not believe his ears and insisted that they go before a *beit din* so that he could repay his debt. Again, Reb Ya'akov won in the *beit din*.

Shlomo was confused by the actions of Reb Ya'akov. What did he mean that he had been repaid by *HaShem?* He meditated on this question for many days until the answer came to him: *it was God he owed!* Afterward, he repaid that debt by helping those in need. His concern for his reputation dissolved, his pride disappeared, and when anyone thanked him, he would only respond, "It is not me you should thank."

Reb Levi Yitzhak finished his story and smiled. "Now you see why Reb Ya'akov deserves such high praise, and why I wanted to follow him to his final resting place. I wanted to share the joy of heaven in his reception on high. I wanted to give thanks to the One who should be thanked for the deeds and the life of such a *tzaddik*. For his life was a foretaste of the days of the *Mashiah* (Messiah). The Torah is eternal and will exist even in the days of the *Mashiah*, and so will dealings between people; but in those days, only law cases like Reb Ya'akov's will be presented."[1]

In the *Mishneh Torah*, the RaMBaM (Maimonides) outlines eight degrees of *tzedakah* (charity).[2] Among the three higher degrees are giving anonymously, giving in such a way that one does not know to whom they give, and giving that turns the recipient into a giver. Reb Ya'akov in his own way, managed to achieve all three in Hasidic fashion, denying any knowledge of his gifts, and by the strange circumstances this brought about, turning his recipients into givers! Today we might call this story, 'Paying it forward.'

New Laws

Reb Levi Yitzhak did not only decide on disputes between litigants, but was also informed and consulted before any new laws were passed in the community of Berditchev. This *ma'aseh* tells of one such 'new' law that was presented to the *rebbe* . . .

One day, the head of Berditchev's Jewish community sent a messenger to Reb Levi Yitzhak to inform him that the Jewish community council was ready to promulgate a new law. So the *rebbe* put on his coat and followed the messenger back to the meeting-house of the council to hear the new law. He entered and everyone stood, waiting for him to take his seat. Then the leader of the council arose with evident solemnity and read aloud the council's proclamation, "Henceforth, shnorrers (beggars) shall not go from house-to-house asking for aid, but shall come to the meeting-house of the council, where they shall be given aid from the funds raised by a new communal tax for the poor." Hearing this, Reb Levi Yitzhak stood and began to put on his coat to leave. The leader of the council, noticing, called out to him, "Rebbe, why are you leaving?" To which the *rebbe* replied, "You said this was a *new law* . . . This is not a *new law*. It is an old law. It comes from the days of Sodom and Gomorrah," and he walked out. The new law was abandoned.[1]

How right he was: this is an "old law." We see it again and again, year after year, and seem to struggle with it more and more as the years pass. Back when we lived in friendly neighborhoods, in houses with front-porches that we sat upon, when neighbors and people in the street actually knew one another, if someone fell through the cracks in the larger social system, there was always somebody around to see it, and who was willing to help them out.

Instead of demanding that people refrain from begging in the streets, we should see what we can do to help the poor and the homeless. Look at the disparity between what we spend on war and destruction and what we spend on health, education and welfare for our fellow human beings; it is so fantastically great— is not this a lack of kindness? It is easy to hear Reb Levi Yitzhak speaking to us today, telling us that we need to bring about some changes in our lives and our values. Most importantly, we need to increase the amount of kindness in our lives—beginning with ourselves, with the members of our family, and the people in our immediate vicinity—and step outside the profit-making mindset to unblock the flow of energy and goods, so it can circulate to the places in our social body that most need it. If our neighbor needs something, we should be able to offer that to them naturally, and then receive back from them just as naturally. In this way, the social fibers will be strengthened and the body of the planet will be healed.

The Test

Reb Levi Yitzhak also had a wonderful way of chiding people about their spiritual lives . . .

Once after Minhah, the mid-day prayers, Reb Levi Yitzhak went around to three Hasidim who were talking after prayers and said, *"Shalom aleikhem,* Reb Aizik! *Shalom aleikhem,* Reb Nosson! *Shalom aleikhem,* Reb Dovid!"* The men were surprised and said, "Rebbe, you greeted us before prayers and we have been here this whole time!" *"No-o-o-o,"* Reb Levi Yitzhak said in a mock-serious tone, "during the Amidah you were in Kiev, Reb Aizik . . . Reb Nosson, you were in Kovno . . . and you, Reb Dovid, you were in Tluste!"[1]

This was all in the spirit of training the awareness of his Ḥasidim and was not meant to embarrass them. Like every good *rebbe*, he was also known to test people now and again, and this next *ma'aseh* is of that genre . . .

A Merciful God

One Sukkot, there were no *etrogim* to be found in Berditchev. The people were almost in despair over the situation when a rich man traveling through Berdichev was noticed to have his own *lulav* (palm frond) and *etrog* (citron).

"A miracle!" the people said, and quickly assailed the man and prevented him from leaving town. "We didn't get an *etrog* here; you must stay and let the *rebbe* purchase it from you and then we'll all say the blessing over the *rebbe*'s *etrog*."

The rich man said, "I'm sorry, but I don't wish to stay, and I don't wish to sell my *etrog*. I only want to get home to my family and to have the *mitzvah* there." But they continued to press him until he finally said, "Leave me alone!"

Then he tried to get away, but they seized him and shlepped him to the home of Reb Levi Yitzhak, who said to the rich man, "If I share with you my part in the *Olam ha-Ba,* the World-to-Come, will you do it?" What could he say? The rich man agreed to stay in Berditchev and share the *etrog*.

Reb Levi Yitzhak then called the *shammes* and told him to spread the word to everyone in Berditchev who had a *sukkah* (holiday booth)—no one is to have the rich man as a guest!

Soon the rich man applied to his innkeeper, "May I eat in your *sukkah?*"

He said, "No, you are forbidden to come into my *sukkah.*"

The rich man goes from *sukkah* to *sukkah* and no one will invite him in. Finally, he learns that it is by the command of the *rebbe* and so he goes to confront Reb Levi Yitzhak and says, "What's this all about?"

"Well," said Reb Levi Yitzhak, "it's very simple; I'll let you eat in the *sukkah* if you give me back my place in the World-to-Come."

Now the rich man felt cheated and angry, but it was Sukkot, and one must eat in a *sukkah.* Grudgingly, he said in a sullen tone, "Alright, I give it back to you . . . You don't owe me anything."

"No thank you," Reb Levi Yitzhak said, "you can keep my place in the World-to-Come! Come into my *sukkah*—you don't have to give anything back—I just wanted to see if you were the kind of person who cares more about a *mitzvah* than the World-to-Come; such a person I want to have in my *sukkah!*"[2]

That is to say, 'If serving God with the next *mitzvah* is more important to you than the reward of the next world, then I want to get to know you, and

A Merciful God

you are welcome to my place in the World-to-Come!'
You see, the Hasidic rebbes went to the opposite
extreme of the admonishing preachers of the
period who continually sought to bring people into
religious observance by promising fabulous reward
or unbearable punishment on the other side of this
life. The Ba'al Shem Tov saw that such conformity
would always be shallow, and that one could only
find depth by abandoning all thought of reward.

For the Sake of Heaven

The previous *ma'aseh* is also an example of how the Berditchever Rebbe was always trying to highlight the holiness of the ordinary person, putting it in the context of the highest service to God, which brings us to the following Torah . . .

A person who puts their heart into the word of God, accepting the yoke of awe *(yirah)*, placing themselves in the presence of God—*shiviti Y-H-V-H l'negdi tamid* (Ps. 16:8)—serves the creator with every movement that they make.[1] Even in mundane physical activities, if one remembers the eternal and true aim, these activities serve as tools for the soul. For this reason, such a person is eager for their work and activity, pursuing it with diligence and discernment, so that every action should be pure and in accord with that which the *Ribbono shel Olam* requires. When such a person studies Torah, every movement of mind and body, according to their capacity, seeks purely to sift and clarify understanding of that which God has commanded. Likewise, when this person is occupied with business, it is as if Torah was the real occupation, in as much as the person is continually paying attention to what the Torah has to say about business.

In some ways, there is nothing startlingly original about this passage. Apart from the emphasis on *kavvanah* (intentionality), it is basically the rabbinic ideal of the householder-priest that was established in Yavneh in the 1st Century C.E.. Nevertheless, it is somehow re-infused with life here by Reb Levi Yitzhak, perhaps because he really believes in it. Of course, he knows that whatever the acknowledged ideal, the sad reality in his time spoke of a rigid separation between the sacred and the profane, declaring work a tiresome necessity and the busy worker an unfortunate ignoramus. But the Berditchever also knew that *kavvanah* was the great leveler, and if he could disabuse the learned of their inflated sense of superiority, and the ignorant of their spiritual roughness and sense of inferiority, justice would prevail among the people, and a previously unknown divine service would ensue.

Reb Levi Yitzhak was especially concerned to found study and prayer fellowships—*ḥavurot*—for ordinary Jews in his community with varying degrees of access to spiritual teaching.[2] He also founded groups for like-minded individuals, those in the same trade, keeping the same hours. Thus there was a bakers' *ḥevrah*, a tailors' *ḥevrah*, a merchants' *ḥevrah*, and in this way, new insights and applications of Torah could come from the common experience and group-mind, which they would then take back into their work-places, just as Reb Levi Yitzhak describes. This is something we need to do again today, whether it be guild-type *ḥavurot* of professors in the humanities, research scientists, writers, business people or computer coders. Of course, it need not be so rigid, but the idea still applies today, even if few of us are tailors or bakers anymore.

Now the opposite type of person will only follow their own urges in the way of all physical things, with no *kavvanah*, no inner intention to serve God at all; all that such a person is interested in is to fulfill these urges. There will not be any internal obstacle to keep them from straying into crooked paths, because their intention is simply to get what they are lusting for, and not to let go of it until the desire is fulfilled. This has two negative results: first, the soul is harmed in the transgression of the *mitzvot;* second, even if they are studying Torah continually, if it be without spiritual motive or out of selfish motives, then this person has not even studied Torah while being seemingly occupied with it! Whereas the other person, even if engaged in business, is entirely occupied with Torah.[3]

A Merciful God

This is a terrible blow to the culture of learning and *Torah lishmah*, 'Torah for its own sake,' for Reb Levi Yitzhak audaciously classes the activity of a spiritually unconscious Torah scholar with the venial desires of an ordinary person, occupied with lust and gluttony! The common denominator is self-interest and a lack of *kavvanah l'shem shamayim*, 'intention for the sake of heaven.' This is as applicable today as it was then, only today, we would frame it a little differently.

Abraham Joshua Heschel, a direct descendant of Reb Levi Yitzhak (and his representative in our time) put it this way (paraphrasing): Today, many of the ultra-Orthodox have stressed the supremacy of Torah, equating it with the *Shulhhan Arukh*, the code of Jewish law, but have nevertheless disregarded the coordinates of God and Yisra'el, and thus have frequently become involved in a kind of religious behaviorism![4] This is really true, and echoes as if it had come from the mouth of his illustrious ancestor.

In all this, Reb Levi Yitzhak shows a genuine concern for the ordinary Jew like no one since the Ba'al Shem Tov. This Torah should be reviewed again and again, for few teachings are so applicable to our situation today. We live in a time-contracted world, and therefore, we must activate our *kavvanah* like never before in the space of our work and ordinary lives, making every inch of it an offering to God.

The White Letters
of the Torah

As Reb Levi Yitzhak was the most prominent 'social activist' among the rebbes of his time, we might not find it all that surprising that he is also the author of what might be called an example of early 'feminist' Torah, in as much as it has profound implications for future teachings on the divine feminine.

"All songs, poems and scripture are written like brick on open space, open space on brick."[1]

At first, we are amazed to see that it is written in scripture, "A new Torah will come forth from me,"[2] as this seems to contradict one of the Thirteen Principles of Faith which states that this Torah will not be changed, nor will another Torah from the creator.[3] However, we may understand this in the following way . . .

A Merciful God

Early Hasidism is especially concerned with the idea of "new Torah," treating Torah as a living process, aided by the continuance of prophecy through a cultivated receptivity to *ru'aḥ ha-kodesh*, 'the spirit of holiness,' all of which we see in the Torah and *ma'asiot* (stories) of the Ba'al Shem Tov and the Maggid of Mezritch.[4]

It is well-known that the letters of the Torah are as inner lights which have come into outer-manifestation through the devolution and unfolding reification of the worlds *(olamot)*. Surrounding the black letters of Torah is white space, which represents the surrounding light that is not given to manifestation, remaining hidden and implicit. From this we may understand that the light of these spaces is as the black letters of the alphabet, but remains hidden next to these manifest letters. It is for this reason that it is forbidden for the black letters to touch one another in the Torah; for if they were to touch, they would obscure and impinge upon the hidden light of the white spaces.

At the splitting of the Reed Sea, we experienced a miracle that transcended nature. At that time, there was revealed a light and a life coming from God which is well beyond the order of devolution; rather, it comes from the category of the surrounding light.

The White Letters of the Torah

Therefore, the Song of the Sea (Exod. 15) is written as brick-work—white on black and black on white—for at that time there occurred a unification of the figure and the ground together, and the white letters became momentarily visible like the black letters.[5]

In Torah, every letter must be free-standing and black. These letters are seen as "black fire" in a white field. The white field, Reb Levi Yitzhak tells us, is also made of "letters," but these letters are not visible to us because it is difficult for a person to see both the figure and the ground at the same time. As in certain graphic puzzles, you might see two black-silhouetted faces on either side of the picture or a white cup in the center, but to see both is very difficult for our perceptual-cognitive apparatus. This has to do with *apperception* as distinguished from *perception*.

Perception has to do with focus; for if we focus on the figure of the two faces, then the white cup is merely the ground, and vice versa. Only recently have we gotten into the idea of the figure-ground reversal; but that is still perception, a choice of focus. Ground over figure, feminine understanding over masculine, will yield new understanding, but it will still be a choice of focus. The goal in the end must tend toward apperception: awareness of the choice of focus and the possibility of seeing both at the same time!

A Merciful God

This is why the Sages, of blessed memory, have said "a maidservant present at the splitting of the sea saw more than Yehezkel (Ezekiel) saw of the chariot," for the manifestation was so vast that even a humble maidservant was able to behold the great theophany.[6]

This is the meaning of the sentence, "A new Torah will come forth from me," for in the future (when the *Mashiah* comes), there shall be a manifestation of God such that all flesh shall see the glory of it. That is to say, there will be a manifestation of the transcendent, surrounding light, and then, the hidden letters will emerge from the white spaces of the Torah. In this way, "A new Torah will come forth from me"—"new" only in that the white letters that have been hidden there from the beginning will then become visible.[7]

In the end, the seeming contradiction with the Thirteen Principles of Faith is solved by pointing out that the 'white letters' are implicit, as if emergent properties in what already exists. But this Torah is much greater than the simple resolution of an apparent contradiction. It is a revolutionary teaching, paving the way to a "new Torah" of the divine feminine. It is amazing to think of this revolutionary teaching being contained in a book that is revered by so many people who would find this idea anathema.[8] But this too is a figure-ground relationship. For those who come across this Torah with an ultra-Orthodox frame and focus will likely fail to see the feminine ground in it, explaining it in a conventionally acceptable way. And that would not be wrong; but it does not do justice to the full import of the teaching either. We must be willing to look at this teaching as pointing to a figure-ground reversal that is necessary for us today. The black letters of the divine masculine Torah have taught us much; but why should we fear *more* Torah from the white letters of the divine feminine?

The description of the "brick-work," the white light surrounding the black letters, can be compared in sexual terms to "the woman surrounding the man," *nekeivah tesovev gever* (Jer. 31:22),[9] which makes it abundantly clear that these white spaces are a feminine container.

Up to now, we have not had a strong influx of feminine input into Torah, except through the Kabbalah, and that has mostly been channeled through men. The channeling through women, I am sure, will bring new subtlety and life even to the teachings of the Kabbalah. That is not to say that these teachings in the Kabbalah are not true teachings of the divine feminine. They are, but it may be that the female biological perspective and cultural context will yield a new understanding of the kabbalistic texts. Moreover, the new influence of women in kabbalistic discourse will yield new root metaphors for our understanding of Torah.

Nevertheless, this will need to be cultivated. For even though there are many women entering the rabbinate today, the demands that are being made of them to be considered valid as rabbis (by both men and women) is that they should master the tradition's masculine form of knowledge. This is not bad thing in itself, but if these 'black letters' should somehow obscure the 'white letters,' because we have left no room for the feminine, then we will have created a flaw in the Torah of the future. Thus, as we embark together on this new journey together, we must continue to honor the bodily inheritance of women and the oral transmissions they have received from their mothers, aunts and grandmothers.

How will this new Torah be integrated into a *halakhah* or law of the future? We have two whole orders of the Mishnah that do not (with small exceptions) have any *gemara* or commentary.[10] The idea of a women's commentary on these fills the mind and heart with joy!

But how are we to understand that these 'white letters' will not be perceivable until the coming of the Messiah? I would want to adjust this a bit by saying, *"with* the coming of the Messiah." It seems to me that the Messiah is always coming, being that quality of progressive redemption that we can see in history. Thus, the 'white letters' are slowly being revealed over time. But I would want to say more than that. The Talmud occasionally says, "This is a great law; but this is a law for when the Messiah comes." It is called, *hilkheta l'meshiḥ* a "the law when the Messiah will come." Now, my friend and colleague, Rabbi Arthur Waskow reads this, "If you want the Messiah to come, then you have to begin behaving as if the Messiah had already come" And this is what we have seen already in the "Three Din Torahs."

The Rebbetzin's Kavvanah

Some of the 'feminine Torah' that is now coming to light is actually being reclaimed from the past. Rabbis Leah Novick, Tirzah Firestone and Ruth Gan Kagan[1] have been responsible for some of this; others like Elisa Klaphek have reintroduced us to Regina Jonas, the first female rabbi and her Torah;[2] and Dinah Berland has produced an English translation of Fanny Neuda's book of prayers for women from nineteenth-century Germany.[3] This work of reclamation is of great importance, and so we make this small contribution, remembering the holiness of Reb Levi Yitzhak's wife, Rebbetzin Perl . . .

It is said that whenever Rebbetzin Perl, the wife of Reb Levi Yitzhak of Berditchev, kneaded the dough and baked the *hallot* for Shabbat, she would pray this prayer . . . *"Ribbono shel Olam,* I pray in your blessed name that when my husband, your servant, Levi Yitzhak says the blessing over these loaves on Shabbat, his mind should be filled with the intentions that fill my own as I knead and bake them in this very hour."[4]

Rebbetzin Perl's own *kavvanah* we are not told, but we can assume it served the divine purpose at the rebbe's *tish* (table). One might suspect that it was something her husband was not likely to have in mind himself, but which would add dimension to the blessings over the *ḥallah*. Even if it were as simple as a desire for health, healing and delight to come from the bread, a nurturing and maternal influence would enter the otherwise exclusively male *tish*.

It was the same when I was a *yeshivah bokher* (student) in Lubavitch. The Rebbe's wife, Rebbetzin Nehamah Dinah Schneersohn (1882-1971) would come to the *yeshivah* refectory on a regular basis to check on the quality of the food. She saw this as her domain and one of her own contributions to the life and health of the community, a way in which she elevated our Torah study.

Teyk"u

In the same way as Reb Levi Yitzhak's teaching on the 'white letters of the Torah' supports the idea of a 'feminine Torah' hidden in the spaces between the black letters, this teaching called Teyk"u supports the notion of paradigm shift, in that God's grace recognizes the need for a continual refinement of our understanding of Torah and the resolving of our doubts. Thus, new answers are continually available to us through the agency of Prophet Elijah . . .

Why do the Rabbis promise that all questions will be answered by Eliyahu ha-Navi when he comes to announce the *Mashiah* and not by Moshe himself, who will be resurrected at that time?

Moshe died and we cannot hope to be helped in our current problems by Moshe, peace be upon him, who completed his life.

TeYK"U is an acronym for *Tishbi yitaretz kushiyot v'iba'yot*, which means, Elijah "the Tishbite will come" and answer our difficult questions. Given that this would occur after the coming of the Messiah (when Moses will be resurrected), it would seem that we could have brought these questions directly to Moses, our teacher, through whom the Torah and the *mitzvot* first reached us. So Reb Levi Yitzhak asks, why should he not be the one to answer the difficult questions? We are simply told at this point that it is because Moses died to this plane of reality, while Elijah did not, having ascended to heaven while yet living. (2 Kings 2:11)

Since that time, the Torah has been placed in our hands, and if one's soul is from the side of grace *(hesed)*, everything is pure, permitted, and kosher, and if it is from the side of rigor *(g'vurah)*, the opposite holds true. Yet each person according to their own rung is a vehicle for the word of the living God. This is why the Sages, realizing the need for grace in this world, set the *halakhah* (law) down according to the teachings of Hillel, for this is according to the world's need.

Here we have the dispute between the generations, it is the argument between Rashi and Rabbeinu

Teyk"u

Tam concerning the *t'fillin*.[1] In this argument, Moses seems to be in agreement with Rashi, but Rabbeinu Tam is not persuaded by this, arguing that the Torah has been given to us, and it is for us to teach and rule on how we understand the sacred Torah today.

Now, when we encounter the holy arguments of Hillel and Shammai, the Talmud states, "The words of *these* and the words of *those* are the words of the living God." (Eruvin 13b)[2] This is because it depends on the temperament and inclination of the person who studies the statement in the holy Torah. If one is rooted in the world of grace and kindness *(ḥesed)*, everything one studies, one sees as if it were permitted, proper and pure; for such a person reads the holy Torah through this inclination of the mind. And we can easily recognize in this the 'frame' of Reb Levi Yitzhak. But the opposite is one who is rooted in the attributes of severity *(g'vurah)*, for they see everything through that particular lens. Now, the school of Hillel was rooted in the attribute of grace and kindness *(ḥesed)* and therefore, all their decisions leaned toward compassion, whereas the school of Shammai, using the attribute of severity *(g'vurah)*, ruled in the direction of conservative restriction. In this way, "the words of *these* and the words of *those* are both the words of the living God." They are just perspectives meant to serve a particular purpose.

When our Sages, of blessed memory, who lived after the generation of the schools of Shammai and Hillel, realized that the world needs to be governed by the attribute of kindness, they anchored the law according to the rulings of the school of Hillel, going in every situation toward leniency.

Now, one who is alive in this world is aware of the needs of the time and the attributes we need to live by. But one who is not alive on this plane does not know the attributes we need to live by in this world. Since Eliyahu is yet existing and alive, never having tasted the taste of death, remaining connected to this plane, he is suited like no other to resolve our doubts.[3]

Here we come back to the argument of Rabbeinu Tam, that it is in *our* hands and not those of Moses to decide the law. This is because, as we said before, Moses completed his life thousands of years ago, and cannot know the unique needs of our lives today. But Elijah, according to our tradition, is still alive, never having tasted the taste of death, and continues to visit this world. Therefore, he is capable of responding to our questions with compassion for the world in which we live today. For only one who is alive in our world can know the way in which our world needs to be governed. But one who is no longer alive could not possibly know this.

Teyk"u

How does this help us if these questions will only be answered after the Messiah comes? This is another example of how the tradition is continually in dialogue with itself, and sometimes working around itself. For kabbalists believe that TeYK"U *(Tishbi yitaretz kushiyot v'iba'yot)* refers to the transcendent insight that they receive in their prayer and meditation, and sometimes to direct guidance received from Elijah in a visitation. Thus, the Kabbalah has been the source of new answers for millennia, and continues to be the well from which the entire tradition is refreshed.

Sweetening
One Last Judgment

Reb Levi Yitzhak's entire life was dedicated to the 'sweetening' of judgments, bringing leniency to a harsh situation out of his great compassion. He was truly from the root of grace and a true heir of Hillel. Thus, in his last years, he was the arbiter of various disputes that had begun to arise between Ḥasidim. In one of the most grievous, the Shpola Zeide, Reb Aryeh Leib of Shpola (1725-1811), began to attack and vilify young Reb Nahman (later of Bratzlav) (1772-1810), who was then living in Zlatopol near Shpola.

In this dispute, Reb Levi Yitzhak of Berditchev came to the aid of Reb Nahman, saying, "If the world would listen, I would cry aloud in a voice that could be heard from one end of the universe to the other, that whosoever wishes to be upright and to serve the Lord in truth should attach himself to Rabbi Nahman."[1] Throughout Reb Nahman's life, he would have no greater defender among the rebbes then Reb Levi Yitzhak. And in this regard, the following dream seems significant.

Reb Nahman recorded various dreams, some of which have been preserved. The following is a report of a dream from his last years . . .

> It was Yom Kippur, the Day of Atonement,
> and I dreamed. It was very clear to me that
> in heaven they demand one person's life
> as a sacrifice every Yom Kippur. Thus, I
> volunteered; but they said that I must put it in
> writing. So I wrote it out and signed it. Then
> they wanted to offer me up as a sacrifice; but I
> now had regrets and wanted to hide. I saw that
> a large group of people had gathered around
> to witness the sacrifice and I could not hide. I
> then sought to leave the city; but even as I left
> it, I noticed that I had somehow just returned!
> I entered the city thinking I might hide among
> the non-Jews. Nevertheless, I knew if they were
> to come searching for me, I would be given up
> to be sacrificed. Then another *tzaddik* agreed to
> be a sacrifice in my place. Still, I am afraid of
> the future.[2]

Now, a *ma'aseh* of Reb Levi Yitzhak's last days
that seems related to the dream of Reb Nahman of
Bratzlav . . .

At the close of Yom Kippur, Reb Levi Yitzhak of
Berditchev emerged slowly from the *beit midrash*
and said to the Hasidim gathered around him, "I

must tell you, dear ones, today my life-line has finally expired and I should be departing this world, even within this very hour; for I am the sin offering of Yisra'el. Nevertheless, I was aggrieved upon learning this because it meant that I would miss the opportunity of fulfilling the *mitzvot* of dwelling in the *sukkah* and saying the *b'rakhah* (blessing) over the *etrog* one last time. Thus, I prayed that my sentence should be commuted until the completion of Sukkot, and the creator has granted my request."

It was as Reb Levi Yitzhak said—the day after Simhat Torah, the holy Berditchever Rebbe suddenly fell ill and died a day later.[3]

Reb Levi Yitzhak of Berditchev died on the 25th of Tishrei, 1809 (5570). Reb Nahman of Bratzlav died the next year on the 18th of Tishrei, 1810 (5571). Whether Reb Levi Yitzhak was the *tzaddik* who sacrificed himself for Reb Nahman or not is for you to decide, but the synchronicity of these two stories is suggestive and seems consistent with the life of Reb Levi Yitzhak.

The hour that Reb Levi Yitzhak died, a *tzaddik* in a far away city suddenly interrupted his discourse to his disciples, saying, "I can't go on; all is dark before my eyes and the gates of prayer are closed—something must have happened to Reb Levi Yitzhak of Berditchev."[4]

In Bratzlav, two days later, Reb Nahman began to speak to his disciples about the departure of a *tzaddik,* the Glory of Yisra'el, from this world. He said, "Surely it is possible that there was a pillar of light going before his coffin, for the true leader of Yisra'el has died. He who has eyes in his head knows that the light has gone from the world and darkness has enveloped us all." The following week, the news reached Bratzlav of Reb Levi Yitzhak's death. Then the disciples knew that Reb Nahman had been speaking of Reb Levi Yitzhak, whom he often referred to as the "Glory of Yisra'el."[5]

Dudeleh

Though Reb Levi Yitzhak departed this world, his legacy has not. Among Ḥasidim, Reb Levi Yitzhak is a *rebbe* for the ages whose life is seen as a model of holiness and whose writings are studied by all, from the lowliest Ḥasid to the most celebrated rebbes. In death, as in life, he stands above the fray and factions, an arbiter transcending all sectarian arguments, a defender of all Israel. He stands above it all because his focus is always on God, surrounding and permeating all things. For him, the words of the Psalmist, "Where can I flee from your presence?" (Ps. 139:7) were a tangible reality, and he celebrated this fact. Thus, it seems only fitting to end with his famous "Dudeleh," his 'You-song' of love to God. To sing it with him is to attune to his spirit and to bring a little of his holiness into our day.

O *Ribbono shel Olam,*
Master of the Universe,
I want to sing You a *'Dudeleh'*
A little song of You!
You! You! You!
Only You!

A Merciful God

Where can I find You?
Where could I not find You?
You! You! You!
Only You!

Wherever I go—You!
Whenever I stand—You!
If all goes well with me—You!
Heaven forbid, if it goes badly—You!
You! You! You!
Only You!

To the East—You!
To the West—You!
To the North—You!
To the South—You!
To Heaven—You!
To Earth—You!
Below—You!
Above—You!
You! You! You!
Only You![1]

The *kever* of Reb Levi Yitzhak. Photo by Zalman Schachter-Shalomi, 2004.

Reb Zalman wearing the *t'fillin* of Reb Levi Yitzhak.

Notes

Beginnings

1. Samuel H. Dresner, *Levi Yitzhak of Berditchev: Portrait of a Hasidic Master*, 18. This wonderful book is highly recommended for anyone who would learn more about Reb Levi Yitzhak's life, prayer, and teaching, as is Arthur Green's later book, *Defender of the Faithful*.

2. Dresner, *Levi Yitzhak of Berditchev*, 18-19.

3. For more on the Maggid of Mezritch and Shmelke of Nikolsburg, see Zalman Schachter-Shalomi and Netanel Miles-Yepez, *A Heart Afire: Stories and Teachings of the Early Hasidic Masters*, chapters 6-9.

Divine Games

1. The Maggid chose to read the sentence, "God said, 'Take your son up for a sacrifice,' not 'Go and sacrifice your son.'" This is a wonderful teaching, for this is always the issue about divine guidance. What did you hear? When we 'hear' God we must listen well and actively to discern the truth of what is being asked of us. Is not that what the word *sh'ma* means, to listen with focus? This reading was suggested by Rabbi Bahir Davis.

2. *Tikkunei Zohar*, 56: 91b.

3. *Sh'muah Tovah* bound with *Kedushat Levi*.

4. See Schachter-Shalomi and Miles-Yepez, *A Heart Afire*, 197-201 for more of the Maggid on the scaling down of ideas.

5. Ibid., 198, 199, 237-38 for the parental analogies of the Maggid.

6. Levi Yitzhak of Berditchev, Kedushat Levi, Parshat Terumah.

A Hasid for a Son-in-Law

1. "It has been clearly demonstrated to you that the LORD alone is God; there is none beside Him.'" — Deuteronomy 4:35. *JPS Hebrew-English TANAKH*.

2. See Martin Buber, *Tales of the Hasidim: The Early Masters*, 203-04 "He Who Was Also There."

3. See Dresner, *Levi Yitzhak of Berditchev*, 22.

Splendor of the Face

1. Samuel Horodetzky, *Ha-Ḥasidut V'ha-Ḥasidim*, 74.

2. See Schachter-Shalomi and Miles-Yepez, *A Heart Afire*, 155-160 "Words and Reality."

The Troubles of a Tzaddik

1. See Dresner, *Levi Yitzhak of Berditchev*, 34-35; the same point is made by Reb Elimelekh of Lizhensk about Reb Levi Yitzhak in Buber, *Tales of the Hasidim I*, 232 "Rabbi Elimelekh's Answer."

Levi Yitzhak, 'the Merciful'

1. Likewise, in the Gospel of Luke 6:36, it says, "Be merciful, just as your Father is merciful." *The Precise Parallel New Testament*, 335.

Notes

2. See Dresner, *Levi Yitzhak of Berditchev*, 40; Buber, *Tales of the Hasidim: The Early Masters*, 221-222 "His Second Name."

Head and Heels

1. This is the phrase Reb Levi Yitzhak continually uses to introduce his points in *Kedushat Levi*.

2. Levi Yitzhak of Berditchev, *Kedushat Levi*, Parshat Ekev.

3. See Miles Krassen's *Uniter of Heaven and Earth: Rabbi Meshullam Feibush Heller of Zbarazh and the Rise of Hasidism in Galicia*.

4. Most of Hasidism and Hasidic rebbes tend to agree.

The Darkened Shell

1. A story remembered by Rabbi Zalman Schachter-Shalomi, *z"l*.

Whole-Hearted Prayer

1. Levi Yitzhak of Berditchev, *Kedushat Levi*, Likkutim.

2. As translated in my own prayerbook. — Z.M.S-S.

3. Levi Yitzhak of Berditchev, *Kedushat Levi*, Pirkei Avot, Perek 2.

4. Talmud, Shabbat, 59b.

5. In Levi Yitzhak of Berditchev, *Kedushat Levi*, Kiddushah Sh'niah, we find:

> The way in which a *tzaddik* serves God in thought brings about a change and influx in all the worlds. Therefore, Mordecai, whose mind was completely connected with God's (in which all things are created for God's glory, including this world), was

A Merciful God

able to effect the light of the first thought of creation unto the very last manifestation of the world of nature. Therefore, even the world of nature fights our battles and causes the downfall of our enemies, as the miracles in Mordecai's time show. This is why Haman and his ten sons were hung through 'miracles' dressed completely in the natural order.

So you can see that that all the worlds begin to light up because of the *kavvanah* (intention) of the *tzaddik* of the generation. Therefore, even the things of the natural world can become greatly refined through them. And then they begin to shine with the original light of creation, when they were created for the sake of Yisra'el, so that they should be able to live in the world of nature, and there experience miracles.

So even though the natural world is the place of external things and energies, in the time of Mordecai and Esther, these were refined through their righteous thoughts.

The Parable of the King's Joy
1. Levi Yitzhak of Berditchev, *Kedushat Levi*, Va-yera'.

Spiritual Audacity
1. Levi Yitzhak of Berditchev, *Kedushat Levi*, Parshat Ekev.
2. C. G. Jung, *Memories, Dreams, Reflections*, 252-53.

The Advocate
1. Numbers 27:15.

Notes

2. Levi Yitzhak of Berditchev, *Kedushat Levi*, Parshat Pinhas.

3. Previously published in Schachter-Shalomi and Miles-Yepez, *A Heart Afire*, xxi-xxii. Also see Martin Buber, *Tales of the Hasidim: The Early Masters*, 222 "The Drayman" for a different telling.

The Small Siddur

1. Dresner, *Levi Yitzhak of Berditchev*, 42.

2. See Dresner, *Levi Yitzhak of Berditchev*, 108.

3. Netanel Miles-Yépez, "The Small Siddur," *Delumin/a: Spirituality. Cuture. Arts.* (Online), May 4, 2015.

Thrice He Won

1. Shlomo Yosef Zevin, *Sippurei Hasidim*, 35-37; Mordechai ben Yehezkel, *Sefer ha-Ma'asiyot*, 378-380. Rabbi Bahir Davis and N.M-Y. both reworked this translation. A version of this was also published previously as Zalman Schachter, "Thrice He Won," *Jewish Heritage*, 23-26.

2. Isadore Twersky, *A Maimonides Reader*, 136-137.

New Laws

1. A story remembered by Rabbi Zalman Schachter-Shalomi, *z"l*.

The Test

1. See Dresner, *Levi Yitzhak of Berditchev*, 101.

2. A story remembered by Rabbi Zalman Schachter-Shalomi, *z"l*.

A Merciful God

For the Sake of Heaven

1. Psalm 16:8: "I have set Y-H-V-H before me always."

2. Dresner, *Levi Yitzhak of Berditchev*, 26-27.

3. Levi Yitzhak of Berditchev, *Kedushat Levi*.

4. Edward K. Kaplan, *Spiritual Radical: Abraham Joshua Heschel in America, 1940-1972*, 361 for Heschel's remarks to the 28th World Zionist Congress.

The White Letters of the Torah

1. Talmud, Megillah 16b.

2. Midrash Rabba, Va-yikra', 13:3. See also "For teaching shall go forth from Me" — Isaiah 54:1 and "See, a time is coming—declares the LORD—when I will make a new covenant with the House of Israel and the House of Judah . . . I will put My Teaching into their innermost being and inscribe it upon their hearts." — Jeremiah 31:31,33. *JPS Hebrew-English TANAKH*.

3. Maimonides' Ninth Principle.

4. See Schachter-Shalomi and Miles-Yepez, *A Heart Afire*, 26-44 "Divine Providence" and 180-92 "The Maggid's Tish and the Transparency of the Teacher."

5. In Exod. 15 it says, "and Miriam took out the timbrel" emphasizing the joy of the feminine. The "brick-work" reference refers to the unique appearance of the text in this passage as it is written in the Torah scroll.

6. Mekhilta, Shirata 3.

7. Levi Yitzhak of Berditchev, *Kedushat Levi*, Tractate Avot.

8. See Moshe Idel, "White Letters: From R. Levi Isaac of Berditchev's Views to Postmodern Hermeneutics," *Modern Judaism*, 169-192.

Notes

9. "A woman courts a man." — Jeremiah 31:22. *JPS Hebrew-English TANAKH.*

10. Zeraim: 1ˢᵗ order only has *gemara* on Berakhot. Toharot: 6ᵗʰ order, only has *gemara* on Niddah, except for the *gemara* Gershon Henokh of Radhzyn added on Toharot.

The Rebbetzin's Kavvanah

1. Rabbi Leah Novick has a book called, *On the Wings of Shekhinah: Rediscovering Judaism's Divine Feminine;* Rabbi Tirzah Firestone is the author of *The Receiving: Reclaiming Jewish Women's Wisdom;* and Rabbi Ruth Gan Kagan located the grave of Hannah Rohel of Ludmir, the first woman *rebbe,* in Israel, and co-authored *Kirvat Elohim* with me in 2006. — Z.M.S-S.

2. Elisa Klaphek, *Fräulein Rabbiner Jonas: The Story of the First Woman Rabbi.*

3. Dinah Berland, *Hours of Devotion: Fanny Neuda's Book of Prayers for Jewish Women.*

4. See Buber, *Tales of the Hasidim: The Early Masters,* 213 "His Wife's Prayer."

Teyk"u

1. There is a story that Rabbeinu Tam, Rashi's grandson, was sitting on Rashi's lap as a baby and grabbed the *t'fillin* off of his grandfather's head. Rashi then said, "Ah-ha, I see that you are going to argue with me over the *t'fillin!*" Years later, Rabbeinu Tam raised the question regarding the proper order of the Torah portions within the *t'fillin.* You see, these portions can be arranged as they appear in the Torah or according to the way in which they make sense with regard to meaning, and thus Rashi and Rabbeinu

Tam argued about which order should be followed. Now since these two great masters are of two opinions, and since the *mitzvah* is of great importance, some people are inclined to wear two different sets of *t'fillin*, one arranged according to Rashi's opinion, and one arranged according to Rabbeinu Tam's. The Ari, Rabbi Yitzhak Luria tells us that it is not because of doubt that we do this, but because of the powerful impact that these variations may make on the soul. Thus, many people (mainly Sefardim) lay two sets of *t'fillin* simultaneously, one according to Rashi, and the other according to Rabbeinu Tam, and others (mainly Ḥasidim) first lay the Rashi style *t'fillin* and then the Rabbeinu Tam. I myself used to *davven* with both the Rashi and Rabbeinu Tam on one strap, and the Lubavitcher Rebbe actually had four pair of *t'fillin* that he would wear for similar reasons of halakhic purity and spiritual effect. — Z.M.S-S.

2. Talmud, Eruvin, 13.

3. Levi Yitzhak of Berditchev, *Kedushat Levi*, Tractate Avot.

Sweetening One Last Judgment

1. Harry M. Rabinowicz, *Hasidism: The Movement and Its Masters*, 100.

2. Eliezier Steinman, *Be'er ha-Ḥasidut: Kitvei Rabbi Nahman mi-Bratzlav*, 168. A version of this was previously published in *Fragments of a Future Scroll*.

3. See Buber, *Tales of the Hasidim: The Early Masters*, 233 "A Period Extended." In Buber, the words about sacrifice are from same year story of Rosh Hashanah, "The Last Blowing of the Ram's Horn." See Dresner, *Levi Yitzhak of Berditchev*, 197-200 "Death of the Rebbe" for a more detailed account.

Notes

4. See Buber, *Tales of the Hasidim: The Early Masters*, 233-34 "The Gates of Prayer"; Dresner, *Levi Yitzhak of Berditchev*, 201.

5. Dresner, 200-01, 218, note 1 translation of *Siḥot ha-Ran*, #196-197 in *Shivḥei ha-RaN*. Reb Nahman's discourse in *Likkutei Maharan Tinyana* #67, 68.

Dudeleh

1. The translation of Reb Levi Yitzhak's lyrics from the Yiddish is difficult to make work in English, so we have made the Dudeleh more like an English poem. For another version in English, see Dresner, *Levi Yitzhak of Berditchev*, 106-07.

Bibliography

Hebrew Works

Horodetzky, Samuel. *Ha-Ḥasidut V'ha-Ḥasidim*. Vol. 2. Tel Aviv: The Dvir Co., Ltd., 1928.

Levi Yitzhak ben Meir of Berditchev. *Kedushat Levi*. Jerusalem: Torat Ha-Netzah, 1993.

Mordechai ben Yehezkel. *Sefer ha-Ma'asiyot*. Tel Aviv: The Dvir Co., Ltd., 1955.

Schachter-Shalomi, Zalman, and Ruth Gan Kagan. *Kirvat Elohim*. Yediot Ahronot, 2006.

Steinman, Eliezer. *Be'er ha-Ḥasidut: Kitvei Rabbi Naḥman mi-Bratzlav*. The Institute for Kabbalah and Hasidism.

Zevin, Shlomo Yosef. *Sippurei Ḥasidim*. Tel Aviv: A. Tzioni Publishing House, 1959.

Hasidic and Kabbalistic Works in English

Buber, Martin. *Tales of the Hasidim: The Early Masters*. Trans. Olga Marx. New York: Schocken Books, 1947.

—. *Tales of the Hasidim: The Later Masters*. Trans. Olga Marx. New York: Schocken Books, 1948.

Dresner, Samuel H. *Levi Yitzhak of Berditchev: Portrait of a Hasidic Master*. New York: Hartmore House, 1974.

Firestone, Tirzah. *The Receiving: Reclaiming Jewish Women's Wisdom*. San Francisco: HarperSanFrancisco, 2003.

Idel, Moshe. "White Letters: From R. Levi Isaac of Berditchev's Views to Postmodern Hermeneutics," *Modern Judaism*. Vol. 26, No. 2, May 2006.

Krassen, Miles. *Uniter of Heaven and Earth: Rabbi Meshullam Feibush Heller of Zbarazh and the Rise of Hasidism in Galicia.* Albany: State University of New York Press, 1998.

Novick, Leah. *On the Wings of Shekhinah: Rediscovering Judaism's Divine Feminine.* Quest Books, 2008.

Rabinowicz, Harry M. *Hasidism: The Movement and Its Masters.* Northvale, NJ: Jason Aronson, 1988.

Schachter, Zalman. "Thrice He Won." *Jewish Heritage.* Vol. 6, No. 1, Summer, 1963.

Schachter-Shalomi, Zalman, and Netanel Miles-Yepez. *A Heart Afire: Stories and Teachings of the Early Hasidic Masters: Revised Edition.* Rhinebeck, NY: Adam Kadmon Books, 2017.

Non-Hasidic and Non-Kabbalistic Works

Berland, Dinah. *Hours of Devotion: Fanny Neuda's Book of Prayers for Jewish Women.* New York: Random House, 2007.

JPS Hebrew-English TANAKH: The Traditional Hebrew Text and the New JPS Translation. 2nd ed. Philadelphia: The Jewish Publication Society, 1999.

Jung, C. G. *Memories, Dreams, Reflections: Revised Edition.* Ed. Aniela Jaffe. Trans. Richard and Clara Winston. New York: Vintage Books, 1989.

Kaplan, Edward K. *Spiritual Radical: Abraham Joshua Heschel in America, 1940-1972.* New Haven, CT: Yale University Press, 2007.

Klaphek, Elisa. *Fräulein Rabbiner Jonas: The Story of the First Woman Rabbi.* Trans. Toby Axelrod. San Francisco: Jossey-Bass, 2004.

Bibliography

Kohlenberger, John R. III, ed. *The Precise Parallel New Testament.* New York: Oxford University Press, 1987.

Twersky, Isadore, ed. *A Maimonides Reader.* New York: Behrman House Publishers, 1972.

Glossary

ahavah (love) – Love, often paired with fear/awe *(yirah)*.

Amidah (standing) – The prayer of *atzilut* in the Jewish liturgy, the eighteen benedictions recited three times daily; on *Shabbat* and *Yamim Tovim*, the *Amidah* has only seven benedictions.

avodah (service) – Often used as a synonym for prayer, as in *avodah sh'b'lev* (service of the heart), or as in *shlemut ha-avodah* (true and complete service) to God.

Barukh HaShem (blessed is the name) – A statement or expression of gratitude to God.

beit din (house of judgment) – A Jewish court of law made up of three *dayyanim* (judges).

beit midrash (house of study or investigation; also *beit ha-midrash)* – Place for religious services and study.

b'rakhah (pl. *b'rakhot)* – Blessing.

bimah – dais.

binah (understanding) – The second or third of the *sefirot* (divine emanations).

bokher (unmarried youth) – A poor student or an unmarried youth.

da'at (knowledge) – Intimate knowledge; an intermediary *sefirah* very important in the ḤaBaD system of thought.

davven (pray), *davvenen* (prayer, praying) – More colloquial way to speak of *t'fillah* (prayer); and yet *davvenen* is also more than formal prayer, or prayer as a formality; it is living the liturgical life in truth. The word itself is possibly derived from the Latin *divinum*, 'the divine,' as in doing divine work.

dayyan (judge) – A judge of Jewish communal affairs.

A Merciful God

d'veikut (adhering, clinging) – Intimate absorption in God, adhering, sticking, or clinging to God in deep devotion and love.

etrog (citron; pl. *etrogim)* – A citrus fruit ritually employed during the holy day of Sukkot.

ga'on (pride, splendor; pl. *ge'onim)* – Genius; a title given to an exceptionally brilliant talmudist.

gevalt – An expression of surprise, dismay, or wonder.

g'vurah (strength, severity) – One of the ten *sefirot,* also called *din* (judgment).

goyim (nations) – Non-Jews.

ḤaBaD (wisdom, understanding, knowledge) – An acronym for three specific s*efirot—hokhmah, binah, da'at;* the name of a Hasidic school of thought and practice, as well as a lineage founded by Shneur Zalman of Liadi (1745–1813).

ha-ala'at ha-middot (raising up of the emotions) – The practice wherein the devotee overcomes temptation by pursuing a stimulus to its most sublime source in the divine.

halakhah (way to walk) – The process; Jewish law.

HaShem (the name) – A term for God, used in place of the unpronounceable name, *Y-H-V-H.*

Ḥasid (one who is pious) – A member of the Hasidic movement; a person who has a Hasidic *rebbe.*

Ḥasidim (pious ones) – Followers of the third religious movement by that name, founded by Yisra'el, Ba'al Shem Tov in the 17th century. The earlier Ḥasidim were the desert Ḥasidim mentioned in the Talmud, the Ḥasidim ha-Rishonim, and the Ḥasidim of medieval Germany, followers of Yehudah HeḤasid, the Ḥasidei

Glossary

Ashkenaz, and the Sufi-influenced Egyptian Hasidism of Avraham Maimonides in the 13th century.

hasidut (piety) – Hasidism, the teachings of the Ḥasidim.

hesed (lovingkindness) – One of the ten *sefirot*. Also known as *gedulah* (largesse).

hevrah (sing. *haver)* – Fellowship.

hod (glory) – One of the ten *sefirot*.

hokhmah (wisdom) – The first or second of the *sefirot* (divine emanations).

kavvanah (intention, aiming; pl. *kavvanot)* – Intentionality, spiritual concentration invested in the service of God.

k'lippah (shell, husk; pl. *k'lippot)* – A metaphysical husk or shell formed around and obscuring a spark *(nitzotz)* of divinity; a synonym for the energy system of evil.

Kiddush (sanctification) – The prayer of sanctification recited over wine on the Shabbat and festivals.

l'shem shamayim (for the sake of heaven) – The attitude which a Ḥasid takes toward sacred activity.

Ma'ariv (evening prayer) – The evening prayer service.

ma'aseh (deed, work, story; pl. *ma'asiot)* – A story of deeds in the Hasidic tradition; the outermost garment of the soul.

maggid (speaks) – An endowed or itinerant preacher of sermons; an early title for Hasidic rebbes.

mahshavah (thought; pl. *mahshavot)* – Thought, the innermost garment of the soul.

mahshavot zarot (strange thoughts) – Disturbing thoughts, especially during prayer.

malkhut (kingdom, sovereignty, majesty) – One of the ten *sefirot*, specifically representing the feminine, the

A Merciful God

Shekhinah.

mamash − So-being-ness, palpable.

mashal (parable; pl. *meshalim)* − An analog or parable used in teaching.

Mashiaḥ (anointed) − The Messiah.

middot (attribute; sing. *middah)* − Emotional attributes of divinity; the modes of being, investment, attitude, and affect. Generally correspond to the lower seven *sefirot.*

midrash (interpretation; pl. *midrashim)* − A method of interpreting Torah; a collection of such interpretations.

Minḥah (gift) − The afternoon prayer service.

mitnagged (opponent; pl. *mitnaggedim)* − An opponent of the Ḥasidim, anti-Ḥasid.

mitzvah (connection; pl. *mitzvot)* − A commandment or God-connection in the Jewish tradition, popularly equated with a good deed.

netzaḥ (victory) − One of the ten *sefirot;* denotes effectiveness.

niggun (melody; pl. *niggunim)* − A Hasidic melody, often wordless, which Abraham Joshua Heschel once described as "a tune in search of its own unattainable end."

olam (pl. *olamot)* − The world, universe.

olam ha-ba (the world to come) − heaven, paradise.

rav − A city's chief rabbi and authority on legal matters.

reb − A term of respect and friendly admiration.

rebbe − The spiritual leader of a Hasidic community.

rebbetzin (rabbi's wife) − A rabbi's or rebbe's wife.

Ribbono shel Olam (master of the universe) − An appellation for the divine.

Glossary

ru'aḥ (spirit, breath) – In kabbalistic terminology, the spirit in human beings; the emotive function of the soul.

ru'aḥ ha-kodesh (spirit of holiness) – The holy spirit, also the *Shekhinah*.

sefer (pl. sefarim) – Book.

sefirot (expressions; sing. *sefirah*) – The ten divine emanations or attributes that manifest themselves in the four worlds; the lower seven *sefirot* are the same as middot.

Shaḥarit (dawn) – The morning prayer service.

Shalom aleikhem (peace be unto you) – A greeting.

Shaygetz! (dirty) – This can be applied to a person or used as an accusation.

Shekhinah (dwelling, presence) – The divine in-dwelling, the presence of God in creation.

Sh'ma (hear) – The statement that says, "Hear O Yisra'el, *Y-H-V-H* is our God, *Y-H-V-H* is One."

shnorrer – Beggar, sponger.

shofar (horn) – Ram's horn blown on Rosh Hashanah as part of the ritual.

siddur (order) – A Jewish prayer book.

simḥah (joy) – Joy; a joyous occasion.

sukkah (booth) – Temporary hut constructed for Sukkot.

tallit – Prayer shawl.

talmidim (disciples) – In this context, disciples of the *rebbe*.

t'fillah – Prayer.

t'fillin – Small leather boxes attached to the head and dominant arm for prayer, containing scrolls with Exod. 13:1–10, 13:11–16, Deut. 6:4–9, 11:13–21.

t'hillim – Psalms.

t'shuvah (turning) – Repentance, penitence.

A Merciful God

tiferet (beauty) – One of the ten *sefirot.*

tish (table) – The public table of the *rebbe;* ritual meal with the *rebbe.*

Torah (instruction) – Specifically the five books of Moses, but generally any Jewish teaching.

tzaddik (the righteous one; pl. *tzaddikim)* – A term for a saintly, righteous person, a charismatic leader, and particularly for a Hasidic leader or teacher, a *rebbe.*

tzedakah (righteousness) – Charity.

tzimtzum (contraction; pl. *tzimtzumim)* – The concealment or self-concealment of God.

yeshivah (pl. *yeshivot)* – An advanced academy for studying Torah, especially for the training of rabbis.

yesod (foundation) – One of the ten *sefirot.*

yetzer ha-ra (evil inclination) – A negative impulse; the opposite of the *yetzer ha-tov* (positive impulse).

Yid (sing. dimin. *Yiddeleh;* pl. *Yiddelakh)* – Jew.

yirah (awe) – Awe/fear, often paired with love *(ahavah).*

Yisra'el (God-wrestler) – The community of Jews and the mythic landscape of Judaism.

Zalman Schachter-Shalomi, widely considered one of the world's foremost authorities on Hasidism and Kabbalah, was a rabbi and scholar of psychology of religion, as well as the founder of the Jewish Renewal movement. He was professor emeritus of Jewish Mysticism and Psychology of Religion at Temple University, and later the occupant of the World Wisdom Chair at Naropa University.

Netanel Miles-Yépez is an artist, philosopher, spiritual teacher, and scholar of religion. Currently, he is the Chair of Religious Studies at Naropa University and the Director of the Keating-Schachter Center for Interspirituality at the university.